The VNR Concise Guide to

BUSINESS LOGISTICS

VNR CONCISE MANAGEMENT SERIES

The VNR Concise Guide to
BUSINESS LOGISTICS

VNR CONCISE MANAGEMENT SERIES

Edited by
Carl Heyel

VNR **VAN NOSTRAND REINHOLD COMPANY**
NEW YORK   CINCINNATI   ATLANTA   DALLAS   SAN FRANCISCO
LONDON   TORONTO   MELBOURNE

Van Nostrand Reinhold Company Regional Offices:
New York   Cincinnati   Atlanta   Dallas   San Francisco

Van Nostrand Reinhold Company International Offices:
London   Toronto   Melbourne

Copyright © 1979 by Litton Educational Publishing, Inc.

Library of Congress Catalog Card Number: 79-4187
ISBN: 0-442-23402-3

All rights reserved. No part of this work covered by the copyright hereon may be reproduced or used in any form or by any means—graphic, electronic, or mechanical, including photocopying, recording, taping, or information storage and retrieval systems—without permission of the publisher.

Manufactured in the United States of America

Published by Van Nostrand Reinhold Company
135 West 50th Street, New York. N.Y. 10020

Published simultaneously in Canada by Van Nostrand Reinhold Ltd.

15 14 13 12 11 10 9 8 7 6 5 4 3 2 1

Library of Congress Cataloging in Publication Data

Main entry under title:

The VNR concise guide to business logistics.

   (VNR concise management series)
   Includes index.
   1. Business logistics.   I. Heyel, Carl, 1908-
HD38.5.V15   658.7   79-4187
ISBN 0-442-23402-3

CARL HEYEL, *Editor*

Management Counsel, Manhasset, New York, and editor *The Encyclopedia of Management*
Formerly Adjunct Professor, Industrial Management and Industrial Marketing, The Polytechnic Institute of Brooklyn

COLIN BARRETT, *Advisory Editor on Traffic and Distribution Subjects*

Transportation Consultant, Reston, Virginia

L. CLINTON HOCH, *Advisory Editor on Plant Location and Industrial Districts*

Executive Vice President, The Fantus Company, Location Consultants, South Orange, New Jersey

VNR CONCISE MANAGEMENT SERIES

This volume of the Van Nostrand Reinhold Concise Management Series, as are all of its companion volumes, is for those executives and potential executives who find that they have to broaden their horizons beyond their own specialities if they are to advance in management. To this end, it has been edited to meet the needs of the person who seeks to acquire a grounding in the basic concepts of a management discipline foreign to his or her area of expertise, but who does not have the time or desire to plow through the detailed expositions and practice exercises in books edited for practitioners. At the same time, the volumes in the Series serve as admirable references and "concept updaters" for those professionally trained in the fields covered.

The chapters in each volume have been prepared by experts in the subject matter covered, and originally appeared as entries in the best-seller Heyel *Encyclopedia of Management,* also published by Van Nostrand Reinhold. However, all of the entries have been supplemented, revised, and updated by Mr. Heyel as required, in collaboration with the original authors or other recognized authorities.

Acknowledgments

As indicated in our opening statement, the chapters in this volume, which appeared originally in the *Encyclopedia of Management*, have been updated and revised as necessary. It is testimony to the excellence of the basic presentations in the original encyclopedia entries that aside from certain statistical information no significant changes have been dictated by the passage of time since the second edition of *The Encyclopedia of Management* appeared in 1973.

Original authorships and affiliations at the time of writing are shown below. However, special appreciation is expressed here for the extensive encyclopedia contributions by J. L. Heskett, 1907 Professor of Business Logistics, Harvard University Graduate School of Business Administration, on business logistics and specifically the case example on the Transportation Problem (using the "distribution solution") included here in the Appendix; and by Nyles V. Reinfeld, Director, National Institute of Management, Inc., on inventory management.

1. Approaches and Techniques: J. L. Heskett, 1907 Professor of Business Statistics, Harvard University Graduate School of Business Administration, Boston, Mass. **2.** Plant Location: Leonard C. Yaseen, Chairman, The Fantus Company, New York, N.Y. **3.** Industrial Districts: L. Clinton Hoch, Executive Vice President, The Fantus Company, New York, N.Y. **4.** Purchasing: Walter E. Willets, Editor, *Purchasing* magazine, New York, N.Y. **5.** Value Engineering: Anthony R. Tocco, Director, Product Assurance Systems, TRW Systems, Redondo Beach, Calif.,

Past National President, American Society of Value Engineers. **6.** Vendor Rating: A. V. Feigenbaum, President, General Systems Company, Pittsfield, Mass. **7.** Material Management: H. B. Maynard, President, Maynard Research Council, Pittsburgh, Pa. **8.** Inventory Management: Nyles V. Reinfeld, Director, National Institute of Management, Inc., Wellington, Ohio. **9.** Physical Distribution Management: Colin Barrett, Transportation Consultant, Reston, Virginia; and (re. shippers' associations) Stephen Tinghitella, Editorial Director, *Traffic Management,* New York, N.Y. **10.** Packaging: Bernard F. Major, Manager, Package Development Laboratory, Ortho Pharmaceutical Corporation, Raritan, N.J.; and (re. protective packaging) Colin Barrett. **11.** Warehousing: Donald E. Horton, Executive Vice President, American Warehousemen's Association, Chicago, Ill. Industrial Distributors: Vijay S. Kothate, Managing Editor, *Industrial Distributor News*, Philadelphia, Pa. *Appendix*: J. L. Heskett.

Acknowledgment is made to the following for reviewing and updating certain encyclopedia entries: George Berkwitt, Editor, *Industrial Distribution,* New York, N.Y., on material-handling equipment types; Alex B. Einbinder, Features Editor, *Industrial Distributor News,* Philadelphia, Pa., on industrial distributors; and Jerry Leatham, President, American Warehousemen's Association, Chicago, Ill., on public warehousing.

Introduction

Business logistics comprises a number of activities for which responsibility traditionally has been fragmented in the operation of business firms. These activities deal with control of incoming and outgoing materials. They include separately identified activities of inbound and outbound transportation, warehousing, materials handling, order processing, inventory control, and supply scheduling. Such activities make up more than 20% of the value of tangible goods produced in the United States.

Formal Definition. The basic function of business logistics is to create "place and time utility" in goods, locating them at the right place at the right time and in the right quantities to meet customer demand. Thus, business logistics can be said to embrace: (1) the management of all activities that facilitate movement, and (2) the coordination of supply and demand, in the creation of time and place utility in goods. The first element of the task, movement control, requires coordinated management of transportation, material management, and storage. The second, demand-supply coordination, deals with order processing, supply scheduling, and inventory management. Each element of the overall task has profound implications for the others. Their planning, activation, and control must be integrated and carried out concurrently.

HISTORY

Business logistics has emerged as a recognized field since World War II. There are a number of reasons for this:

(1) Early emphasis on efficiency in manufacturing and sales left logistics as the last major area of operations in the business firm which had not received concentrated attention. Many feel that the field currently offers potential cost savings greater than either manufacturing or promotion.

(2) The logistics systems of business firms have been greatly complicated by product diversification, the development of new sources of products, components, and raw materials, and the extension of markets geographically.

(3) The field lends itself well to the use of quantitative techniques which have been developed in the past 25 years.

(4) The recent availability of electronic data processing equipment in quantity has facilitated the growth of business logistics by providing the opportunity to mechanize the gathering and analysis of information.

(5) The development of new methods of moving goods in containers, on pallets, by air, or by coordinated systems of two or more modes of transportation has expanded the alternative methods available to the firm in accomplishing its logistics task.

(6) Proponents of the recently-developed *marketing concept* have placed emphasis on a greater attention to customer wants. This in turn has led to broadened product lines and more stringent customer service standards, both of which have created pressures for improved approaches to the management of logistics activities.

Professor Howard T. Lewis of Harvard was one of the first to recognize the potential of a coordinated approach to problems of business logistics in the firm. Early efforts dealt with the establishment of the subordinate field of material management. This first gained acceptance in the air-frame industry, primarily concerning itself with the integrated planning and control of transportation, warehousing, inventories, and often purchasing, of component parts and raw materials. Professor Lewis' study, "The Role of Air Freight in Physical Distribution," coauthored with James W. Culliton and Jack D. Steele and published in 1956 by the Division of Research of the Harvard Graduate School of Business Administration, was the first full-scale attempt to present currently accepted concepts. Business logistics has since been widely adopted by many business firms.

Early development of concepts of business logistics occurred in the distribution of grocery products, biologicals, pharmaceuticals, chemicals, cleaning agents, toilet preparations, and other products. Common characteristics of such industries are the production and distribution of products which require (1) balance between sizeable charges for logistics services and (2) high customer service standards.

Subject Branchings. Business logistics is made up of an amalgam of management activities and organizational functions which have existed for many years. At the heart of these is material management, physical distribution management, and traffic management. In addition, industrial engineering has supplied some of the approaches through its attention to materials handling in production, transportation, and storage of goods. Other specific branches of the subject are order processing and production scheduling, inventory management, and warehousing. (The first-named is treated in Chapter 9, PRODUCTION PLANNING AND CONTROL, of the companion volume of this series, *Industrial Management*; the other two in Chapters 8 and 11 of the present volume.)

For the executive primarily interested in business logistics, and for the executive primarily concerned with industrial engineering aspects of industrial management, there is a certain amount of overlap in subject matter, especially as regards inventory management. Accordingly, for the sake of continuity in subject development and to make each volume logically complete, an editorial decision was made to include identical chapters on value engineering and inventory management both in the present volume and in the volume on industrial management.

Contents

Introduction	xi
1. Approaches and Techniques	1
2. Plant Location	7
3. Industrial Districts	22
4. Purchasing	29
5. Value Engineering	36
6. Vendor Rating	44
7. Material Management	49
8. Inventory Management	60
9. Physical Distribution Management	77
10. Packaging	97
11. Warehousing	107
12. Industrial Distributors	116
Appendix—Case Example: The Transportation Problem (Using the "Distribution Solution")	123
Index	133

The VNR Concise Guide to
BUSINESS LOGISTICS

VNR CONCISE MANAGEMENT SERIES

1
Approaches and Techniques

Basic to the field of business logistics is the *movement system concept*. Its underlying principles include: (1) viewing the movement of goods not as an activity carried on by or for one firm, but by and for all firms in a channel of logistics; (2) analyzing all costs resulting from the use of one of many methods of accomplishing a logistics task; and (3) designing a system involving personnel, machines, and information in such a way that the parts are closely integrated to create greater productivity in the system than that claimed for the sum of its parts.

The first of these principles recognizes that the price of a product to an ultimate consumer includes the cost of the sum of a number of logistics operations repeated over and over in a channel of logistics. Thus the separate healths of all firms in a channel are interrelated, requiring that any one firm in the channel analyze a movement system in terms of the logistics techniques employed by its suppliers and consumers as well as itself.

Second, business logistics calls for the appraisal of *all* costs of transportation, storage, material handling, order processing, and the carrying of inventory under all practicable alternatives. This may involve trading one cost for another. For example, a decision to use rapid, premium transportation (such as air freight) might increase a firm's direct costs of transportation and yet give it a lower overall cost by eliminating certain warehouses, reducing inventory levels, and offering lower packaging and packing outlays. A basic objective of total cost analysis, then, is the measurement of *cost trade-offs*.

The concurrent design of all movement system components is rarely possible because of previous commitments and heavy emphasis on sunk costs. However, the third underlying principle of the concept advocates, to the extent possible, the avoidance of *sub-optimization* of system components—that is, the optimization of one system component to the detriment of total system cost or performance.

LOGISTICS SYSTEM ANALYSES

Any analysis of a logistics system will emphasize certain areas of study more than others, based on the definition of the system, the goal of the study, the nature of constraints imposed, the analyst's familiarity with the relative importance of system components, and the likely nature of cost trade-offs. Most analyses to date have been limited to a portion of the product items, product lines, or company divisions of a company under study. Thus, system definition in terms of product, geographical territory, or company division is an important first step in any analysis.

Next, the goal of the analysis should be determined. Is it to cut costs? Is it to improve physical service to customers? Must recommendations result in both? What are the time periods under consideration for goal achievement?

The early identification of constraints on a given study can save much wasted effort. Can plant and/or warehouse locations be altered? Can marketing territories be added, or more especially, can they be eliminated? Does competition require a given level of customer service? Can service levels be adjusted? Will pricing recommendations based upon costs of logistics for varying quantities of product be entertained?

Types of Information. More or less of the following types of information may be required for a given analysis: First, vital data on a company's markets should include the number, location, and size of customers. Service requirements imposed by competition, company policy, or both should be determined for those segments of the market most important to the company. Sales records and interviews can generate much of this type of information.

What is the nature of the product or products for which logistics systems are being analyzed? Important characteristics include: (1) product value, (2) weight, both unpacked and packed for shipment, (3) cubic measurements, both packed and unpacked, (4) the substitutability, in the customer's mind, of competing products for the product in question, and (5) the likelihood of product obsolescence—among others. Products frequently purchased or sold simultaneously can often be treated as one product to simplify analysis.

What is the nature of inventory fluctuations? First, what are sales patterns over a particular period of time, usually a year? Are these caused totally by fluctuations in demand, or are patterns induced by company actions such as promotional efforts, seasonal back-order situations, or product design changes? What production patterns have been followed in the past? In what kinds of procurement patterns has this resulted? What types of inventory fluctuations of both finished goods and raw materials do these patterns typically produce? Are these fluctuations avoidable? Or are they the price of constant production levels or a high level of customer service?

What is the nature of the inventory on hand? Is it balanced with likely demands for various items over order cycle lead times? Or does it conceal dead stocks made obsolete by past inventory control decisions? What purpose does the inventory on hand serve? What portion of it is insurance against short-run back order situations? What portion is necessitated by seasonal demand over longer periods of time?

In order to answer many of the questions associated with inventory management, one needs to estimate the costs of ordering, storing, and transporting various items or product groups. What is the average cost to process a purchase order? What inventory holding costs are associated with raw materials? How do these affect order quantities for various item groups? What effect does the volume transportation rate, when combined with quantity purchase discounts, have on the order quantity inventory policy? How rapidly do suppliers respond to company orders, in terms of order cycle length? What level of transportation service can be expected between various sources of supply and the point of use? How does this affect the reorder point for goods stocked on a fixed reorder point inventory policy? What is the cost to process a sales order?

In addition to those questions associated most directly with inventory policy, others are related to specific areas of activity. How does the price for the purchase of speed, through increased technology in transportation, warehousing, or order processing, compare with the likely savings in decreased inventory and increased sales? What is the comparative dependability of various purchased services, or of company-owned and -operated transportation and warehousing facilities? What levels of accuracy do current order processing systems provide? What costs result from inaccuracy? To what extent can this trade-off be optimized by improved order processing equipment or methods?

Mathematical Programming. The technique of mathematical programming have lent themselves effectively to the analysis of movement systems. One widely used application has come to be known as the Transportation Problem, referring to the use of either the *distribution* method or the *simplex* method of mathematical programming in the pairings of origins and destinations for shipments moving between them. This has resulted in more effective allocation of: (1) production to alternative producing sites, (2) storage to warehousing alternatives, (3) purchases to alternative sources of supply, and (4) finished products to alternative markets. A case example of the Transportation Problem, using the distribution method, is given in the Appendix.

Queueing theory has aided in materials handling. It has been utilized in the design of conveyors, the scheduling of pickup and delivery vehicles into loading and unloading facilities, and other problems of materials flow. It is likely that the use of *mathematical models* to simulate logistics systems will continue to grow. Other techniques related to the field of *operations research* may profitably be used. (See the companion volume in this VNR Series, MANAGEMENT DECISION-MAKING.)

ACCEPTANCE

Business logistics is sometimes referred to as *physical distribution management,* or *physical supply management.* Some experts in the field have variously defined the subject as *distribution management, movement control,* or *rhocrematics.* However, there is a growing trend to consider the field as: (1) encompassing both physical supply and physical distribution management, and (2) the essential link between production and marketing.

An increasing variety of firms recognize the importance of business logistics. A recent survey found logistics departments or divisions in such diverse businesses as farm machinery and equipment, bakery products, automobile manufacture, department stores, petroleum refining, chain store retailing, and others. Of fifty firms studied, forty-one had given new status to the function in the prior three years.

Firms recognizing the potential of improved management of business logistics activities have reported annual savings in costs of up to 3% of sales, with no deterioration of customer service. In addition, the expansion of marketing territories by more effective use of logistics services has led to increased sales. (In many companies, improved customer service was the primary objective.)

The National Council of Physical Distribution Management was organized in 1963 in response to the growing interest in integrated management approaches to logistics problems. The growth and success of this organization has mirrored the increased emphasis placed on the "systems approach" to the management of logistics activities in numerous organizations.

POTENTIAL

The primary deterrent to growth of the field is the lack of fully qualified personnel to deal with logistics problems. A background adequate for the job would generally include some knowledge of the following subjects: mathematics, statistics, traffic management, industrial engineering, purchasing, inventory control, and production planning. In addition, the candidate would have to demonstrate the breadth of viewpoint to take an overall, total cost approach to problems with which he might be confronted.

Major emphasis to date has been placed on problems of physical distribution. The less-popularized area of physical supply management, through universal application of logistics in the operations of a business enterprise, will likely come in for its share of attention in future years. Although its growth will vary from industry to industry, the underlying importance of business logistics is too great to be neglected. As a result, the management of logistics activities which link a firm externally to its suppliers and customers, and which tie the firm's internal functions of purchasing, manufacturing, and sales together, will improve.

2
Plant Location

For many U.S. manufacturing industries, the location of plant facilities can effect a differential of 10% to 15% in total production and distribution costs. Geographic variations in return on investment—always an important consideration—have become even more critical as American companies seek to improve their share of maturing domestic markets and meet the competition of an increasingly industrialized world.

A poor locational choice involves a finality and costliness that can persist for many years. Conversely, a company's profitability can be enhanced and its competitive position strengthened through strategic location of manufacturing capacity.

WHEN TO PLAN

The motivating force behind many new industrial facilities has been management's impromptu response to a "crisis," e.g., immediate need for more capacity, a lengthy strike, an inflationary union contract, a railroad abandonment, a pollution injunction, or new punitive tax legislation. Since inadequate time is available for a thorough exploration of alternatives, locational decisions made in meeting such emergencies can be hasty and ill-conceived.

Good management practice calls for more orderly and systematic planning for new and expanded capacity. Just as careful tracking of competitors' pricing, marketing, and new product development is now standard procedure in most firms, so it has become mandatory to monitor changing competitive relationships in production and distribution costs.

One early warning signal of such cost imbalance is a declining profit margin on the firm's major product lines. Rather than merely reacting to clever competition, management should have a long-term plan for progressive reductions in unit costs through (1) a program of modernization and (2) strategic positioning of its plants and warehouses.

Another continuous sounding must be made for the company's changing competitive position in its local labor market. Declining productivity, extended recruiting time to fill job openings, increased turnover, or excessive absenteeism should be viewed as precursory messages of future labor difficulties. Unless the firm can afford to adjust to inflationary aspects of the local external wage structure (perhaps caused by an influx of new plants), management should be preparing to shift production to lower-cost labor market areas.

Planning for plant location, therefore, must be viewed as a *constant* effort, rather than a response to immediate problems. Only this approach can enable the time-pressed executive to weigh his options and develop an effective production and distribution strategy.

HOW TO PLAN

Good planning for new production facilities begins with a "feasibility" phase in which management's philosophies, objectives, and assumptions are tested against the realities of economic geography. Simulation techniques can be employed to explore the possibilities for accomplishing cost reduction, increasing market share, etc. Use of a production/distribution model allows necessary adjustments to be made in the original specifications and constraints in response to regional cost variables.

In the feasibility phase, the following questions should be considered:

A. What are the costs and competitive implications of the company's present configuration?

   1. Marketing penetration?
   2. Labor availability and cost?
   3. Raw material availability and cost?
   4. Utility supply and cost?
   5. Exposure to environmental controls?
   6. Total operating expense?

B. What are the costs and competitive implications of a change in that configuration?

   1. Can economies be accomplished through
      a. Consolidation?
      b. Decentralization?
   2. If consolidation is indicated, should it be at the present location? At a new location?
   3. If decentralization is indicated, should it be by geographic division or by product line? Which product lines?
   4. What are the nonrecurring expenses associated with each of these alternatives? Is the cost/benefit ratio favorable?

C. Can sales be increased through the addition of branch plants? Should such plants be located in order to

   1. Maximize market penetration?
   2. Neutralize competition?
   3. Minimize unit costs?

D. Is the present physical distribution system yielding optimum results?

   1. Are the present warehouses efficient in number, location, capacity, inventory, and service level?

2. What is the true interrelationship of plants and warehouses?

   a. Can additional branch plants replace distribution warehouses?

   b. Can additional distribution centers eliminate the need for more branch plants?

When goals and strategies are firmly established, management may proceed with confidence into the more advanced phases of site selection.

SELECTING THE REGION

Modern analysis techniques can be readily applied to the traditional factors in location research, assisting in the determination of the most favorable region or subregion. The efficiency of computers not only permits a wider range of alternatives to be considered, but also narrows the geographic area which ultimately must be examined. While some of the examples which follow were developed as solutions to specific problems, they will serve to illustrate the use of mathematical concepts in selecting the optimal region for proposed facilities.

Transportation Costs. Comparative freight cost studies typically consist of extensive tables containing individual rates to and from representative locations, selected more or less at random. The expense of preparing these tables is quite high, and attempts to find the least-cost solution can be laborious. Moreover, quality of the result is highly dependent upon the skill of the researcher in selecting comparison points and his knowledge of territorial rate structures.

Adding to the complexity of the problem, use of published class rates may lead to erroneous conclusions. For any sizable plant, carriers can be expected to establish more favorable commodity rates on key inbound raw material movements and on volume shipments to major markets (or warehouses). While the carriers may be reluctant to commit themselves to lower rates prior to actual plant construction, a realistic estimate of comparative total freight cost is an essential element in the decision process.

A practical method of simplifying freight data has been developed which is useful in plant location analysis and related physical distribution problems. Basically, it permits freight rate trends to be expressed in terms of "best fit" for one of three empirical equations:

$$\text{Type 1} \quad y = a + bx$$
$$\text{Type 2} \quad y = ax^b$$
$$\text{Type 3} \quad y = ax^b + \alpha$$

Based upon tariff research, appropriate trends are identified for published rates, i.e., from raw material suppliers to existing plants in the study area and from regional manufacturers of similar products to their key markets. The computer program establishes the constants (a and b) and derives the adjustment factor (α). Given an input of the distance factor (x) and the total weight to be shipped, it can estimate rates (y) and costs for an infinite number of candidate locations.

Exhibit I illustrates how a computer program was used to determine the least-cost transportation point for a proposed branch plant in the Central States. The area under consideration was divided into 50-mile blocks and the computer established total shipping charges on a finished product to a 15-state market region from the center of each block. It also constructed isobars of inbound freight cost from six alternative raw material sources. On the final printout, block "38-H" was identified as the least-cost location, with annual charges of $181,500. The range extended to $322,000 within the study area, and the program defined the penalties in each of the 48 blocks for later use in evaluating potential offsetting variations in other cost factors.

Still another plant location problem solved by computer techniques considered not only the optimum cost of serving present markets from alternate locations, but also programmed: (a) projected increases in the volume of sales and extent of market penetration through improved delivery schedules; (b) variations in

12 VNR CONCISE GUIDE TO BUSINESS LOGISTICS

Exhibit I
Base Map—Combined Transportation Costs

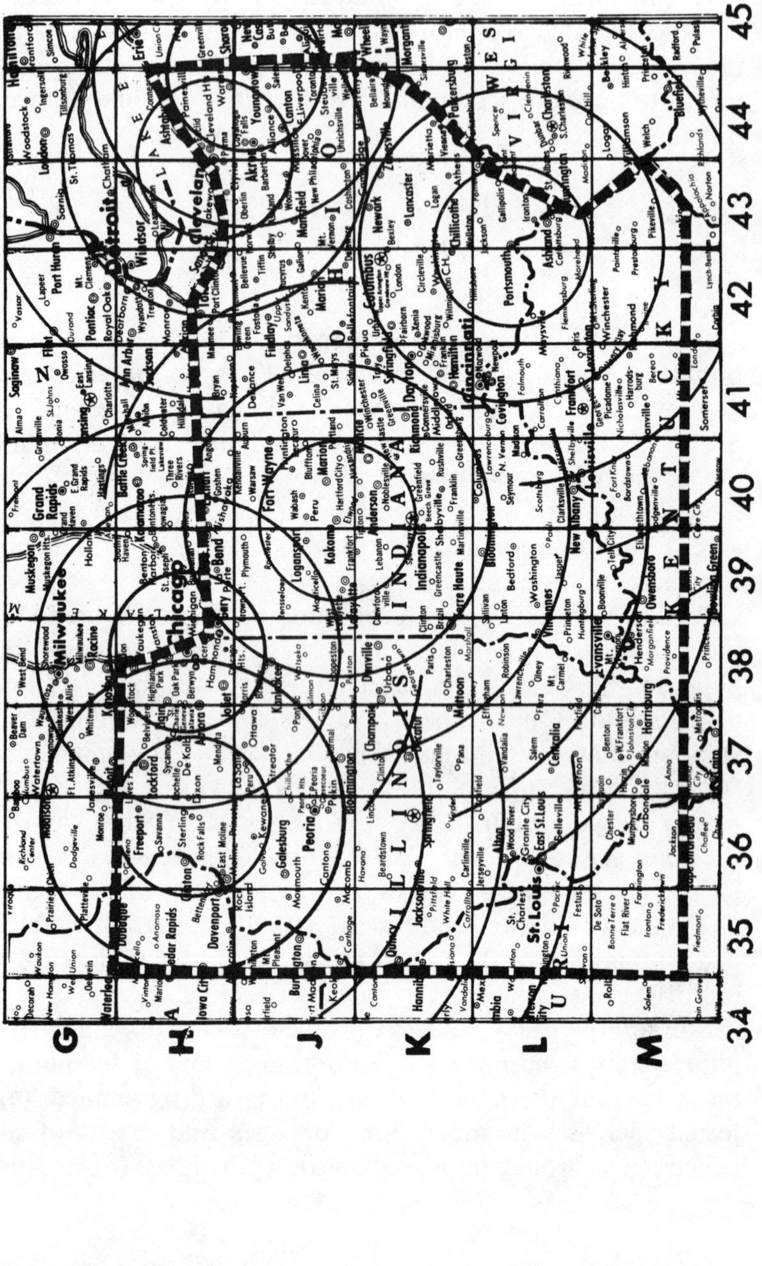

growth rates among present and future customers; (c) anticipated inflation in freight rates; and (d) projected gradual changes in the unit weight and other characteristics of the product itself.

Warehouse Location. Attempts to apply usual Operations Research techniques to the warehouse location problem are frequently unsatisfactory. Since the primal-dual algorithms are designed for "allocation" situations, they cannot be correctly utilized in studies where the number of warehouse facilities, their size, and their geographic position are completely flexible. Configuration of physical distribution networks is best treated as a mathematical relationship between freight rates applying from origin plant(s) to service territories.

Exhibit II provides a graphic illustration of these relationships, which determine both the *size* and the *shape* of the area that can be economically served from any selected warehousing point. Contrary to common practice, distribution warehouses should not serve a circular territory.

Trend line A on the graph represents the carload rate on a given commodity from a Midwest plant to potential warehousing points in the East, and line B represents the trend of LTL rates from the origin plant to these same markets. Internal warehousing expense (rent, labor, taxes, interest on inventories, etc.) is plotted vertically as cents per 100 pounds at XY for any selected distribution point.

By shifting the LTL trend to Y as origin, the graph describes the full cost of delivery through the warehouse. Plotted as line C_1, this LTL trend from the distribution depot intersects line B (the direct LTL rate from the plant) at point Z_1. Thus, a warehouse located 400 miles east of the Midwest plant can economically ship stock to markets 825 miles east of the warehouse city.

Reversing the LTL trend line from point Y as origin, plotted line C_2 intersects line B at point Z_2. In the "backhaul" direction, therefore, the warehouse can ship stock economically only for a distance of 40 miles.

Labor. For most manufacturers in older industrial centers of the U.S., payroll costs are outpacing dollar inflation. Under the com-

Exhibit II
Determining the Economics of Warehouse Distribution

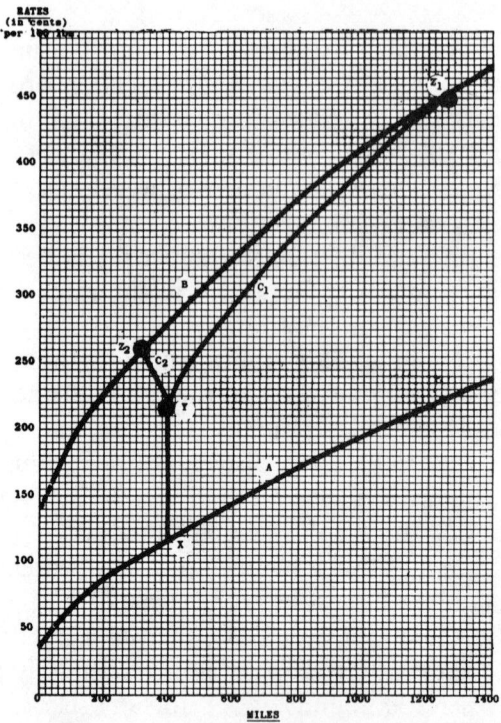

Line A shows carload rate on a given commodity from a Midwest plant to potential warehousing points in the East. Line B is the trend of LTL rates to eastern markets. Warehousing costs are plotted vertically as cents per 100 pounds. Line C_1 is the LTL line shifted to Y as origin. Line C_2 is reversed LTL trend line to determine backhauling costs. Z_1 is the eastern limit for economic shipments for a warehouse located at X, 400 miles east of the plant; Z_2 is the western limit for economical backhauling from a warehouse at X.

bined influence of strong union pressures and periodic labor shortages, wage patterns in these metropolitan areas have been distorted to the extent that unskilled and semiskilled workers have disproportionately high earnings. The net result is disturbing not only in terms of rising payroll costs, but also in the loss of incentive for individual employees to advance their skills. Lagging productivity is further compounded by resistance to improved machinery and manufacturing techniques.

Companies recognizing the situation have effectively minimized payroll costs by moving highly-repetitive fabrication and assembly operations out of their main plants to areas where wages are lower. Removal of simpler work has allowed the parent plant to concentrate on products requiring specialized labor. But, in the process of decentralization, management has frequently discovered that most so-called "skills" can actually be broken down into a series of less complicated tasks, and even highly complex products may be re-engineered to reduce or eliminate specialized labor needs.

Labor costs, of course, play an important role in determining the location for most decentralized operations. Management is seriously concerned, therefore, with the availability of most favorable wage patterns and their long-term stability.

Despite several decades of industrial migration, regional differentials in wage rates have persisted—and even show evidence of widening. Earnings of production workers in the Middle Atlantic and North Central States generally held parallel with the national average, rates throughout most of the South are lower, while the pattern in the West has exceeded the national average. Moreover, the prevalent practice of granting equal *percentage* increases in multiplant companies is reinforcing the persistence of differentials:

	Plant #1 (Northeast)	*Plant #2* (South)	*Plant #3* (Far West)
Average Hourly Rate			
Prior to increase	$6.30	$4.55	$7.05
After 10% increase	6.93	5.01	7.76
Differential vs. Northeast (Plant #1)			
Prior to increase	—	−$1.75	+$0.75
After 10% increase	—	− 1.92	+ 0.83

Computer programs have been utilized to measure industry-by-industry and region-by-region trends in wage rates, fringe benefits, productivity, length of workweek, unionization, etc. These techniques permit the long-term outlook on payrolls to be directly compared with projected inflations among other cost factors and indicate shifting relationships, if any.

Computers have also aided companies to establish appropriate wage postures for new plants entering small communities or semi-rural areas where no comparable employment exists. If wages offered by the firm were too low, recruiting efforts might be unsuccessful in these environments, and dissident employees at the new facilities might resort to job action. If wages were too high, then profits might be unduly curtailed. Utilizing the "wage profile" approach, the computer program simulates the competitive position of the new industry under mature conditions in the local economy. Management is assured that it will be establishing appropriate internal differentials for various skill levels and that plantwide average earnings will be consistent with external conditions of the labor market.

Pollution. The basic premise of the ecologist is that, in order to survive, our economic system must be compatible with the environment. Business leadership must accept that premise, while being astute enough to recognize that compliance costs still show rather sizable geographic variation.

Fiscal attitudes also vary considerably among the states. Some provide partial allowances for costs of pollution abatement equipment. Others offer special amortization and tax credits. A substantial number of states exempt buildings and equipment devoted to air and/or water pollution treatment from ad valorem taxation.

Computers have been helpful in evaluating the alternatives of once-through systems and recirculation, considering the implications on capital investment, utility bills, taxes, etc. Computer-based risk analysis has also been applied to measure the advisability of installing pollution control equipment initially in the new plant or reacting to a threatened injunction at some future date.

SELECTING THE COMMUNITY

In the subsequent site selection phase, the most likely candidates within the designated region are identified. Since this process involves numerous statistical and cost comparisons, the computer again can be a very useful analytical tool. No matter how extensive, however, such tabulations and rankings will have no real value without a comprehensive knowledge of the states and communities under consideration.

Personal field inspections are essential to the evaluation, and checklists are helpful in assuring that no key factors are overlooked. (See below, *Checklist for Site Selection*.) Yet, value judgments will still be necessary in appraising many of the tangible and intangible variables to reach a decision among the leading contenders.

In the field of taxation, for example, states typically apply allocation formulas based upon proportionate shares of property, sales, and payroll. But definition of even these elemental terms can differ radically. Consider the following interpretations of what constitutes "property" in two contiguous states (italics are ours):

State A: "The word 'value' as applied to property other than inventories, shall mean the *original cost* plus any additions or improvements, *without regard to deductions* for depreciation, amortization, write-downs, or similar charges."

State B: "The word 'value' as applied to property owned other than inventories shall mean *original cost* plus additions and improvements *less reserve for depreciation.*"

The interpretation by State A is obviously more beneficial to major multi-plant firms owning fully depreciated property in other states. The denominator of the property ratio will be larger, of course, by applying full original cost to all real estate, resulting in a lower state tax liability.

It is even more difficult to make meaningful comparisons of city and county fiscal data. In almost half of the states, local government accounting practices are not specified by law. Published tax rate tables fail to provide accurate information on local assessment practices and are usually silent on pending revaluation surveys. Most vague are the stipulations with respect to the levels of taxation on tangible and intangible personal property, where permissible by statue.

Similar data problems are encountered in the analysis of school systems. Once considered a reliable indicator of quality, "expenditures per pupil" figures are now distorted by the special needs of inner-city schools, support of court-imposed bussing in rural areas to achieve racial balance, etc.

Personal judgment and objectivity are essential in evaluating such difficult intangibles as "life style," labor stability, and ability to learn industrial disciplines. But even in such prosaic topics as utility rates, workmen's compensation insurance, and unemployment benefits, the researcher must be prepared for hidden clauses that can adversely influence proposed operations.

Finally, the company must be aware of changing community attitudes toward industry. Some basic tenets are being shaken. Securing a new payroll was historically of paramount importance in most areas of the nation, and entire communities would enlist enthusiastically in campaigns to raise money for new plants. Today, citizens may vote just as fervently to eliminate an industry that is "polluting" the environment. In the past, a politician could achieve prominence through a "balance-agriculture-with-industry" platform. Today he may not be elected unless he promises to clean up or shut down these same plants. As a consequence of these changing attitudes, it is increasingly difficult to find communities that truly understand and are willing to provide for industry needs.

Twenty-five years ago, in an article on plant location, Maurice Fulton, location consultant, prefaced his comments by two questions: "What makes for a good plant location? What criteria should management use in selecting a new site?"

He continued by saying: "It depends partly on whom you ask, because different executives have different views and prejudices. But it also depends on *when* you ask. The answer that XYZ Company would have given twenty-five years ago differs from the one it would give today. And the answer it would give today will probably be out of date ten years from now. Top executives who overlook this fact will cost industry hundreds of millions of dollars"[1]

These remarks have been more than confirmed. The contradictions, pressures, and ambiguities involved in the final location decision can be resolved only through constant and increasing research and through the intelligent application of the most modern techniques available.

CHECKLIST FOR SITE SELECTIONS

The following checklist can be used to develop a comparative analysis of candidate communities, sites, and available buildings. Detailed review is necessary to reach an informed decision among the leading contenders.

Community

(1) Population
(2) Location in state
(3) Distance to nearest major city
(4) Description of central business district
(5) Description of residential areas

Transportation

(1) Air access
(2) Rail services, including TOFC ramps
(3) Motor carrier services
(4) Water carrier services
(5) Parcel services
(6) Bus lines

Labor Market

(1) Size of the labor force
(2) Commuting patterns
(3) Labor availability
(4) Present employers
(5) Wage levels

[1] Fulton, Maurice, "Plant Location 1965," *Harvard Business Review,* March–April, 1955.

(6) Fringe benefits
(7) Turnover and absenteeism rates
(8) Productivity levels
(9) Labor-management relations
(10) Vocational training facilities

Utilities

(1) Availability and cost of electric power
(2) Availability and cost of gas
(3) Price of alternate fuels
(4) Capacity of water system and rates
(5) Capacity of sewer system and rates
(6) Chemical analysis of water supply
(7) Regulations on waste disposal

Municipal Services

(1) Number of policemen and patrol cars
(2) Description of fire protection services
(3) Public schools, statistics and quality
(4) Hospitals and accreditation status

Taxes

(1) Current tax rates, city and suburbs
(2) Assessment practices
(3) State taxes, corporate and personal

Living Conditions

(1) Housing availability, purchase and rental
(2) Recreation facilities
(3) Cultural facilities
(4) Religious facilities (including parochial schools)
(5) Climate

Supporting Services

(1) Hotels and motels
(2) Restaurants
(3) Financial institutions
(4) Post office
(5) Telephone company
(6) Machine repair and industrial supply
(7) In-plant feeding services
(8) Continuing education courses

Incentives for Investment

(1) Financial assistance
(2) Tax moratoriums and credits
(3) Training assistance
(4) Site preparation, etc.

Sites

(1) Size and description
(2) Foundation conditions
(3) Flood hazards
(4) Zoning
(5) Road access
(6) Rail access
(7) Utility lines, size and position
(8) Tax rate
(9) Ownership
(10) Asking price

Available Buildings

(1) Size and description, including land area
(2) Ceiling clearance and bay size
(3) Floor, thickness and surface condition
(4) Zoning
(5) Truck loading facilities
(6) Rail siding capacity
(7) Utilities services, transformers, etc.
(8) Taxes
(9) Ownership
(10) Asking price or rental quotation

3
Industrial Districts

In older manufacturing centers, industry is plagued by cramped sites, traffic congestion, and inadequate parking facilities. Preference for single-story plants, coupled with the desire to avoid future congestion, has directed attention to the planned industrial district. This is a tract of land subdivided and promoted by a sponsoring managerial organization for industrial occupancy. While the term "industrial park" is used increasingly as a promotional device, it would be misleading to give any definitive status to that title.

Industrial districts vary considerably in their extent of planning, but the basic concept provides for the installation of streets, railroad tracks, and utilities before sites are sold (or leased) to industry. Building and zoning restrictions are frequently adopted to protect the character of the district and future real estate values. In its most advanced form, the planned industrial district may offer a full range of services: assistance in design, financing, and construction; fire and police protection; banking; restaurants; club rooms; computer time-sharing; etc.

TYPES OF DISTRICTS

Characteristics of a planned industrial district will depend, in large measure, upon the promoting group and its objectives. Some general observations can be made, however, on the types of districts established by typical sponsors.

Railroad Districts. Railroads create industrial districts in an effort to increase freight revenues. Availability of land in districts of this type, therefore, may be limited to manufacturers or distributors who can guarantee substantial rail tonnage. Carriers are seldom interested in more than a break-even price on the land in their districts (and, were it not for I.C.C. restrictions, some would readily release land below actual development cost). With a few notable exceptions, railroads seldom exercise strict controls over the type of buildings which can be erected, setbacks, ratio of land coverage, or vehicular movements within their districts.

Entrepreneural Districts. Many planned industrial districts are owned and operated as private enterprises for profit by real estate corporations, building contractors, architects, real estate brokers, or syndicates comprising a combination of such interests. This type of district is generally the most highly developed from the standpoint of restrictions, as well as services to occupants. In direct contrast to the railroads seeking additional tonnage, private developers of industrial districts are vitally interested in return on investment. They aim to secure AAA-1 firms as occupants and, under present income tax provisions, they usually prefer to erect structures for long-term lease (rather than sale of raw land).

Community-Sponsored Districts. The basic motivation for community sponsorship of an industrial district is the attraction of new payrolls. Older urbanized areas may also use this type of district to discourage the migration of existing industry. Community-sponsored districts may be organized by the Chamber of Commerce, industrial foundations (profit or nonprofit), local or county governments, port commissions, airport authorities, redevelopment agencies, or special commissions. In some states, legislative approval has been obtained for industrial districts to be financed with statewide industrial development funds—including the erection of speculative buildings.

Industry-Sponsored Districts. Manufacturers themselves have been sponsoring an increasing number of planned districts. These projects may involve a speculative real estate venture on the part of the corporation. More frequently, however, the district represents an opportunity for the industrialist to recoup the costs of developing the site for his own new plant by selling off excess land. The industry-sponsored district may also be used as a marketing tool. In the case of chemical manufacturers, this procedure is adopted as a means of insuring an outlet for products, attracting potential customers for over-the-fence delivery at adjacent sites. Similar motivation has led to the establishment of sponsored districts by steel mills where occupancy is restricted to steel users.

TRENDS

While the concept of the planned industrial district predates the American Revolution, greatest growth has occurred in the United States since World War II. Prior to 1940, only 24 districts had been established; 87 were added between 1940 and 1954; and almost 4,000 are listed currently.

Size of the typical district has also been changing. Most developments created before 1950 contained less than 300 acres. Average size increased to 500 acres during the 1950–60 period, and some were announced which exceeded, 1,000 acres. Current trends indicate a decline in average size, probably reflecting the more intensified land developments of port authorities, inner city agencies, etc.

Considerable design changes can be observed. Increasing use of automobiles and trucks has required larger paved areas for parking and off-street loading ramps. Major thoroughfares within new developments are 60 to 80 feet wide in contrast to the 30-foot widths in older districts. Utility lines are increasing in size and some new districts have completely eliminated overhead wires. Rail crossings are being minimized, and lack of rail access is no longer considered a serious sales deterrent. The average size of buildings in industrial districts has held remarkably constant. Higher ceiling clearances and larger bay dimensions, however, are expanding the average cubic capacity of structures—particularly warehouses designed for modern material handling equipment.

Advantages. The typical occupant of an industrial district is a manufacturer or distributor having need for a small to medium size structure. For smaller projects, management is generally reluctant to develop an independent site which may involve a long rezoning procedure, costly extension of utilities, etc. In the industrial district, appropriate zoning has been obtained by the developer, and all necessary facilities are usually in place prior to construction.

Distinct economic advantages may be available in the form of centralized services: contract maintenance; security guards; restaurants; banking; etc. In addition, covenants may protect real estate investments against deterioration and insure a safe, pollution-free environment. Unquestionably, the availability of risk capital for a "package" or "turnkey" plan has also been an important factor in the growth of industrial districts.

Special advantages can be claimed by the district for warehouse operations. Since the geographic location of distribution facilities is more often dictated by service requirements than cost differentials, the industrial district usually represents a viable site. Moreover, it offers the flexibility of sale or sublease if market conditions change or distribution policies are altered.

Disadvantages. The major objection to industrial districts involves land allocation. In order to pay out, developers of a district must insist upon a high ratio of land coverage, usually 50%. This 2-to-1 ratio of land to building contrasts sharply with the requirements of growing companies for sites having ample opportunity for future expansion. More open acreage may be made available in the district, but only at increased annual rentals equivalent to the income another plant on this land could provide to the developer.

Another major disadvantage of districts is the higher cost of land, whether for sale or lease. In some cases, this may represent an unreasonable price inflation by the owners. More frequently, however, it reflects an inherent problem of industrial districts: "overbuilding." Developers tend to install interior roads and utility lines meeting city specifications so that they may be deeded to the municipality (along with maintenance responsibility) when the district is fully occupied. An industrial company improving its own site, of course, would not attempt to meet such strict standards and could effectively reduce costs.

Similarly, construction costs in many industrial districts can be excessive. In some cases, this situation occurs in the absence of competitive bidding opportunities because the land is controlled by a firm of contractors. More frequently, however, it reflects an attempt by the new occupant to match the expensive design features of neighboring plants in the district. Elimination of "frills" unwarranted by the manufacturing process or warehouse function would reduce costs on an independent site.

By far, however, the most frequent objection to industrial district locations concerns labor, in all its ramifications. It is extremely difficult to establish (and maintain) wage patterns consistent with the needs of each individual firm in an industrial district. National companies operating warehouses or small plants in these development areas frequently offer the same wages and fringe benefits paid in their home plants—wherever they may be located. Consequently, the district may contain a hodge podge of wage structures which may prove disruptive for a manufacturer competing with other producers in his industry who do not face similar problems. For these and other reasons, occupants of industrial districts report comparatively unstable labor management relations. Labor problems can be extremely contagious in such industrial concentrations.

Some industrial districts have unintentionally introduced traffic congestion. Planning within the district may be excellent, but simultaneous release of employees by all occupants at shift change hours may cause congestion at main exits, backing up within the district itself. The concentration of industry also involves considerably more movement of rail cars at grade crossings and heavier truck traffic than would be encountered at an independent site.

RESEARCH AND DEVELOPMENT DISTRICTS

The concept of a planned district for R&D is a relatively recent innovation. Successful marketing by a few districts possessing locational attractions has prompted widespread imitation, and now almost 120 "research park" developments have been established throughout the United States. They range widely in size, from a few acres to over 10,000 acres. Research directors are virtually unanimous concerning the importance of orienting their laboratory facilities to leading universities. It is not surprising, therefore, to find that many planned districts are sponsored (directly or indirectly) by institutions of higher learning. However, a scientific complex of the Federal Government can also be considered a major attractor.

Site requirements for a research laboratory differ significantly from those sought for manufacturing, and these prerequisites can be met in an R&D district if it is planned intelligently. Freedom from noise, odor, smoke, dirt, and vibration is imperative for "controlled-condition" laboratories. Further, the district should be oriented to attractive residential areas, the local university, and a good commercial airport. Since research facilities are relatively expensive to build, the district must also offer prospects for retaining or improving real estate values.

Advantages of the planned R&D district over an independent site primarily involve the economic potentials of centralized services: contract maintenance, security, restaurants, conference auditoriums, etc. The most successful developments offer computer centers, pooling of scientific instrumentation, testing laboratories, technical libraries, and even atomic accelerators.

The primary disadvantage in many planned districts is a restrictive land coverage ratio. The R&D site must be capable of expansion because (1) the full extent of research activity cannot be predicted when the new laboratory is constructed; and (2) the demand for increased laboratory space is often quite abrupt. Research directors in established districts also complain about the noncompatibility of salary and fringe benefit levels in private and government laboratories, especially during periods when corporate budgets are subject to cost pressures.

The greatest danger, however, involves the probability that sponsors will be forced to admit light manufacturing within the district in order to be financially successful. Such mixed use detracts from the R&D atmosphere and can introduce attendant problems of congestion, air pollutants, and higher wage rates for support labor.

OFFICE DISTRICTS

Almost 400 "office park" developments have been established in the suburban sectors of major U.S. metropolitan areas since 1960. Their growth has coincided with the rapid expansion of white-collar employment and the accelerating trend toward decentralization of headquarters and administrative offices. As in the case of the suburban shopping center, a planned office district competes with both the downtown sector and a free-standing structure to be built by (or for) the prospective tenant. To be successful, the developer must offer more than reduced executive commutation, freedom from congestion, lower taxes, etc.—all of which are available at an independent suburban site. He must also be able to demonstrate operating convenience in a protected environment. Increasingly, therefore, developers of office districts offer such built-in services as: covered parking, restaurants, health club facilities, barber shops, retail stores, and helicopter shuttles to airports.

Occupants of planned office districts cite some disadvantages. Rentals, of necessity, are somewhat high in fully-serviced developments. Smaller firms feel a loss of identity in multi-tenant buildings, especially when the structure is renamed for a major occupant. Lower-paying companies report excessive clerical turnover, mostly defections to higher-paying companies in the same district. Among nonexempt employees, common complaints are inadequate public transportation, long walking distances between parking areas and building entrances, and lack of reasonably-priced luncheon facilities.

4
Purchasing

In any commercial transaction, however primitive, there is always a buyer and a seller. Thus purchasing is one of the basic functions in any economy. The buyer requires certain goods and materials to satisfy his wants. He seeks a seller who can and is willing to supply him with what he needs. Together they negotiate a mutually satisfactory price and the deal is completed.

Industrial purchasing is a highly refined, highly specialized version of this activity. Modern manufacturing firms spend, on the average, more than half their sales income on materials, goods, and services purchased from other companies. They assign this buying job to specialists who have the authority to select suppliers and commit company funds.

Purchasing's responsibilities have a direct effect on the company's financial and competitive position. The buyer, in addition to investing his company's money prudently, must satisfy the demands of the operating departments. Thus the "best" price that he constantly seeks involves much more than selection of the lowest quotation.

In selecting a supplier and negotiating a price, the buyer must also be certain that what he is buying will (1) meet specifications and quality standards; (2) arrive in the plant on time to meet production schedules; and (3) be stocked in amounts sufficient to meet manufacturing requirements without causing excessive carrying expense. He must see to it that the supplier gives prompt and adequate service.

Individual purchases can range from simple to highly complex. The buyer of an intricate electronic subassembly for a lunar rocket obviously faces greater problems than the buyer of No. 2 fuel oil. The electronic unit involves advanced engineering and exotic materials. Nothing like it may have ever been made before; neither the buyer nor the supplier has any real cost data to go on in negotiating a price. No. 2 fuel oil, on the other hand is a standard product, with basic specifications. The market price can be found on the business page of the morning newspaper.

More complex purchases obviously require buying experts. It is in the relatively simple purchases, however, that justification for a specialized, centralized, purchasing department can be found. An expert buyer of any commodity will do much more than check current prices. He will study market trends in an attempt to anticipate price changes. He will analyze his supplier's shipping and his own company's storage methods for possible improvements that will reduce costs. He will, for example, study the long-range supply outlook and possibilities of substituting competitive fuels. In such studies, he will work closely with the plant engineer.

Definition. The broad scope of Purchasing's interest and authority requires elaboration on the classic definition: "Purchasing is the activity responsible for getting the right material to the right place, at the right time, in the right quantity, at the right price."

Purchasing—or more precisely, procurement—can be called that function responsible for the phase of the materials cycle from the time an item is requisitioned until it is delivered to the user. This includes direct responsibility for selection of vendor, negotiation of price, and assurance of quality and delivery; it can also include direct or indirect responsibility for transportation, receiving, inspection, and inventory control.

BACKGROUND

Until the turn of the century, the concept of a separate, independent buying function did not exist in American industry. In most cases, company owners did their own buying. As companies grew larger, the buying job was delegated to engineering or manufacturing managers on the premise that those who specified and used materials naturally knew best how to buy them.

As industry expanded, however, and mass production dominated the industrial scene, functional specialization became a necessity. Purchasing agents were named to handle the paperwork of buying. With the advent of World War I, the advantages of having a strong, specialized purchasing department became obvious. With production and engineering managers hard pressed to carry out their own duties, buying was left to buying experts and they performed creditably.

As purchasing men recognized the potential in the function and their own opportunities, they saw the need for making an organized effort toward self-improvement and education. In 1915, a number of local purchasing groups formed the National Association of Purchasing Agents (now the National Association of Purchasing Managers). N.A.P.M. has grown steadily since then to a membership of almost 23,000 in more than 125 local affiliated associations in all parts of the country. The association sponsors a broad range of educational programs through its numerous committees, climaxed by the annual convention each year. The monthly report of its Business Survey Committee on economic and market conditions is widely printed throughout the business press and is used by the U.S. Department of Commerce in its monthly publication *Business Conditions Digest*, as a leading economic indicator.

The purchasing function went through another growth cycle in the twenties and thirties, climaxed by developments in World War II. The advance of mass production and industrialization led to greater emphasis on management of the materials function. The mad scramble for materials during World War II and the period immediately following spotlighted Purchasing's important role in finding and developing supply sources.

The return of fierce competitive conditions in the late fifties and early sixties spotlighted its unique abilities in cost reduction. And throughout both periods, management learned that Purchasing was an integral part of the manufacturing team, along with Engineering and Production. Good purchasing, it was realized, was something more than a mere service function, called in to perform a more or less clerical task after important material decisions were made elsewhere. Purchasing was, in the words of one prominent procurement executive, becoming a "profit-making function."

MODERN CONCEPTS

John H. Hill, president of Air Reduction Company, Inc., speaking before the National Association of Purchasing Agents, put the development of Purchasing in these terms:

"Purchasing traditionally has been considered a service function, a place where money was spent, not made . . . Recent developments have shaken this point of view. Good purchasing is essential to good profits. The difference between good purchasing and poor purchasing can be the difference between outstanding results and mediocre performance. Modernized purchasing departments have shown that skillful procurement can cut 5 to 10% from the total cost of goods purchased.

"A saving of 5% to 10% in the cost of purchases (in a company where purchases absorb 50% to 60% of the sales dollar) is equivalent to 2½% to 5% of the sales dollar."

This concept of procurement helps define the objectives of a modern well-run purchasing department with broad responsibility. *Purchasing Magazine* has listed them as follows: Low prices for purchased materials and services; high inventory turnover; low cost of acquisition and possession; continuity of supply; consistency of quality; low payroll costs; favorable relations with suppliers.

Other objectives of the department include: new materials and products; greater standardization and interchangeability; product improvement and simplification; good relations with other departments; long and short term economic forecasts; reduction of transportation costs; favorable reciprocal relations.

Value Analysis and Pre-Production Purchase Analysis. Value analysis is an organized effort to reduce costs on purchased parts and materials. It involves a study of every part and service to determine how much of its cost could be reduced without impairing its function. Purchasing's success with value analysis led to an extension of the technique to other departments. Value Analysis or Value Engineering, Production, and Purchasing in thousands of plants. (See following chapter.)

Purchasing has also moved up its analytical efforts in many companies to the design stage of a product. At this point it is able to recommend, on the basis of its market experience, changes in design or materials to take advantage of new developments or new techniques available from suppliers. In one major television company, for example, an engineer from the purchasing department participates in design engineering discussions of new or improved products. Thus Purchasing gets involved in the design-manufacturing cycle long before prints are made and handed to it with requisitions.

Vendor Evaluation. With greater demands and greater responsibilities being place on it, Purchasing has in turn taken a closer look at the most important link in the materials cycle, the supplier. Both new and established vendors are coming in for a more critical review of their plant and capabilities, financial condition, and performance. Regular physical inspection of suppliers' facilities by teams from Purchasing, Engineering, and Production are not unusual.

Statistical measurement of vendor performance on price, delivery, and quality has become standard practice in hundreds of industrial purchasing departments. The techniques used vary from the relatively rough approach of asking buyers and using departments to rate suppliers on certain factors, to developing index numbers of performance from data taken from computers. In the latter case, weights are assigned to each category (e.g., Price—40%; Quality—30%; Delivery—30%). Index numbers are calculated for each factor, as well as for over-all performance. (See Chapter 6, VENDOR RATING.)

Inventory Control. Although stores are not always directly under the control of the purchasing department, Purchasing has an important stake in inventory control policy. How well inventory is controlled affects material shortages, the number of purchase orders that must be placed, possibilities of obtaining quantity discounts, expediting, and supplier relations—all Purchasing responsibilities.

Inventory control systems range from relatively simple to very elaborate, depending on the nature, variety, volume, and value of the items involved. A basic step in any system is the segregation of items into three classes: high value, medium value, and low value. (Critical items, regardless of dollar value, are generally placed in the high value category.)

Control procedures are then developed for each category, the stricter controls naturally being placed on the higher value items. This would include frequent review of future requirements, lead time, quantity on hand, quantity on order, safety stock, etc.

The basic objective is to have the right part or material on hand when it is needed. But it is also important to keep average inventory at a minimum, so that carrying costs are kept down and money which could be used productively elsewhere is not tied up in inventory. On the other hand, frequent ordering boosts administrative costs. Purchasing agents therefore try to order in quantities in which ordering costs and inventory carrying costs are in balance, thereby giving them lowest over-all costs. This quantity—calculated through the use of standard formulas—is known as the Economic Ordering Quantity, or EOQ. (See Chapter 8, INVENTORY MANAGEMENT.)

In the past few years, Purchasing has developed a number of techniques to shift some of the responsibility for carrying inventory on to the supplier. These include contract purchasing, blanket orders, "stockless purchasing" programs, and commitment buying. Excluding minor variations, they all involve the same basic approach: to assure a given vendor a certain amount of business in a given period if he will maintain a stock of the item and release it as needed by the customer. This enables Purchasing to avoid piling up an inventory of the item, cut its ordering paperwork, and generally obtain a lower price on the basis of increased volume.

REDUCTION OF ADMINISTRATIVE COSTS

Since the generation of paper is inherent in the purchasing function, close control of administrative costs is of continuing concern to the purchasing agent.

Purchasing has developed a number of procedures and methods designed to reduce clerical effort and costs and free personnel for more creative buying. These range from the universally used traveling requisition to punched card and punched tape systems to handle paperwork involved in repetitive purchasing.

Today Purchasing is also using integrated data processing systems to tie together purchasing, inventory, and production data. Computers are used in the larger companies to store purchase histories, price records, inventory figures, data on suppliers, engineering specifications, accounting records, and receiving information. The equipment is being used to write purchase orders, produce expediting documents, make vendor payments, figure cost data, and measure supplier performance.

As the administrative side of purchasing becomes more automated, its managerial and technical responsibilities will be broadened. Purchasing agents and buyers will have to have greater knowledge of manufacturing operations, materials and processes, and general economics. They will require greater skill in negotiating complex contracts with suppliers. They will have to possess a certain degree of skill in both financial and engineering analysis to evaluate vendors—or have that skill available to them in their own departments. All this in turn will increase the demand for purchasing executives who have a broad concept of the materials function, and the ability to manage every phase of it.

5
Value Engineering

During the years since World War II, value engineering (also known as Value Analysis) has emerged as an effective cost-reduction discipline in defense, space, and consumer products industries.

ORIGIN AND DEVELOPMENT

The genesis of value engineering can be traced to 1947 when the General Electric Company launched an intensive effort to identify the essential functions of their consumer products, and to attain these functions at lowest cost. The term was coined by H. A. Winne, Vice President, Engineering for General Electric, to describe the original set of techniques created for this purpose. Lawrence D. Miles, Manager of Value Services, was given the prime responsibility for the value analysis program, and is credited with its successful development at GE.

A parallel development was taking place in Ford Motor Company purchasing at the same time. Basically, it involved a study of every part and service to determine how much of its cost could be reduced without impairing its function. This included a search for alternate materials or manufacturing processes; elimination of unnecessary features; location of specialty suppliers who could make the part for less; and substitution of standards for specials.

The growth pattern of value engineering can be traced to a number of compelling factors. In the defense industry, the cost-plus-fixed-fee contracting environment virtually ignored cost effectiveness in the mad scramble for superior performance and rapid delivery of weapon systems. Ultimately, the cost spiral reached such proportions that more and more individuals and agencies within the Department of Defense became preoccupied with the task of arresting this trend.

Within the DOD, the Navy Bureau of Ships was the first military establishment to evidence an interest in this new approach to cost reduction. In 1952, the Bureau sent a task team to GE to examine at close range the *what, when,* and *how* of value analysis. Results of this survey were sufficiently encouraging to warrant the initiation of a similar effort in 1954 within the Bureau of Ships. The driving force was Rear Admiral Richard S. Mandelkorn, who organized the first Navy value engineering program. A formal value engineering activity was established early in 1954, and by 1956 all Naval shipyards had a value engineering program under way. For his contribution to this undertaking, the Navy awarded the Navy Distinguished Public Service Award to Miles in 1958.

The development of an effective value engineering program, together with attractive contractual incentives, has enabled the Department of Defense and many of its prime contractors to realize substantial savings. Within nondefense industry, value engineering emerged initially as an effective answer to the cost/price squeeze. More recently it has become an integral cost-reduction discipline in the space program, civil systems, hospitals, construction, and a wide variety of other industries and activities.

Formal Definition. In simplest terms, value engineering is the systematic use of techniques which identify the required function, establish a value for the function, and finally provide the function at the lowest overall cost. It differs from pre-existing cost-reduction activities in that it is *function*-oriented, involving a searching analysis of the function of a product as opposed merely to seeking lower costs in methods and processes to produce the *same* item. Obviously, value engineering involves the use of many known cost-cutting techniques. Organization of these techniques in a manner which permits systematic application to *function* represents, in part, the "newness" of value engineering.

Differences of opinion have existed concerning the definition of value engineering, as regards both philosophy and application. This divergence stems in part from an attempt to distinguish between value engineering and other cost-cutting techniques and disciplines, e.g., work simplification and the various approaches of industrial engineering. Actually, it represents an amalgam. George Fouch, former Deputy Assistant Secretary of Defense (I&L) defined it as follows: "Value Engineering is a managed, purposeful, orderly methodology for increasing the return of an investment on specific targets of opportunity—with no loss in required performance." Officially, the DOD describes value engineering as "a systematic and creative effort, directed toward analyzing each contract item or task to ensure that its essential function is provided at the lowest overall cost."

METHODOLOGY

Five basic phases of the value engineering program constitute what is called the Value Engineering Job Plan, as follows:
   (1) Item selection.
   (2) Information and analysis of function.
   (3) Development of alternatives.
   (4) Analysis of alternatives.
   (5) Proposal development.

Item Selection. An item selected for value engineering study may be hardware, software, a system, or any type of product or service. Carefully considered are such factors as the production quantity, unit cost, timeliness of change in the production cycle, implementation costs (which include not only production-line modifications, tooling, and procedures, but also the effect on spare parts, manuals, field maintenance, etc.), and others.

Some organizations have developed standards of value which provide indicators to areas where low value exists. In such cases a previously established (standard) cost for a given function is compared with the actual cost of that particular function, in a product currently in design or manufacture. For example, value standards have been developed for such functions as generating electric current, interrupting current flow, power transmission, etc. Accordingly, items whose costs are out of line with established standards are natural candidates for value engineering study. (It should be stated that if adequate value standards are lacking, item or project selection is accomplished largely on an intuitive basis.)

Priority of selection is then based largely upon (1) production quantity, current and future; (2) present status with respect to design and/or production; (3) present item value; and (4) implementation costs.

Information and Analysis of Function. In this phase, the objectives are (1) to collect all pertinent information available about the item (e.g., specifications, design criteria, costs, quantity, manufacturing methods, and the like); (2) to determine the item's basic (required) and secondary functions; and (3) to determine the cost of the item and the "worth" of the functions involved.

To accomplish these objectives, the following basic questions must be answered:
(1) What is the item?
(2) What is its function?
(3) What is its present cost?
(4) What is the "worth" of its function?
(5) What else will perform the function?
(6) What will *that* cost?

The design is reviewed with the cognizant design engineer from a standpoint of determining the item's "engineering history"—what approaches were taken; what failed; what succeeded. Manufacturing and purchasing personnel are consulted on the same basis. Finally a complete assessment of the information obtained leads to the determination of required or essential function(s).

In this phase of the study a number of "tests for value" are applied. These are typical:
(1) Does its use contribute value?
(2) Is its cost proportional to its usefulness?
(3) Does it need all of its features?

(4) Is there anything better for the intended use?
(5) Can a usable part be made by a lower cost method?
(6) Can a standard product be found which will be usable?
(7) Is it made on proper tooling—considering quantities used?

Development of Alternatives. This represents the speculative or creative phase of the Job Plan. Having defined the required function, the next step is to examine the methods used to provide this function and to explore alternate approaches. Creative problem-solving techniques are employed extensively in the determination of alternatives. Thus in logical sequence, speculation follows the accumulation of all relevant information and the analysis of function. Again the emphasis is on *function*, a ground rule which allows complete freedom of thought—as opposed to conventional cost reduction efforts which are basically directed toward producing essentially the *same item* at lower cost.

Analysis of Alternatives. Having developed a number of promising alternative approaches to the attainment of essential function, the value engineer now begins to make cost comparisons and other comparative analyses. The lowest cost method is tentatively selected, subject to verification that it will provide the required function and will lead to net reduction in overall cost without degradation of any other essential design parameters, e.g., reliability, safety, maintainability, etc.

Proposal Development. The economically promising alternative approaches are next subjected to intensive technical evaluation, to assure feasibility. In some cases technical adequacy is easily demonstrated; in others proof of feasibility demands considerable effort, often involving hardware testing and verification of results. Finally, a value engineering proposal is generated which presents all data necessary for final evaluation by the cognizant engineering authority. A typical proposal would include design sketches, material and labor costs estimates, tooling requirements, and all other cost consequences associated with the change.

The object of course, is to provide in this document answers to all questions which might arise in the mind of the individual who ultimately must accept or reject the proposal. The fact that executive decisions are often made on the basis of minimum personal risk, represents one of the major roadblocks to cost reduction changes—all the more reason why the value engineering proposal must be "airtight."

APPLICATION AND RECENT DEVELOPMENTS

Since the original value analysis techniques were developed primarily for application to high-production consumer products (such as refrigerators and cooking appliances), the discipline was not ideally suited to the defense environment wherein weapon system acquisition is characterized by low production quantities, rapid state-of-the-art changes, high complexity and high reliability, etc. To meet the needs of this more sophisticated environment, value engineering has undergone changes which have placed the emphasis "up stream" in the specification, design, and production process. Accordingly, a comprehensive value engineering program in defense industry normally includes several specific activities. Each case represents an amalgam (both new and old) of value engineering technology and application. Briefly outlined and described they are:

Specification Analysis. In specification analysis, VE techniques are applied to identify and eliminate areas of "overspecification." The mechanism to accomplish this is a *value oriented specifications review*, wherein the value engineering principles are applied. Check lists are employed which serve to place emphasis on the cost consequences of each specification requirement.

Design Review. Periodic design reviews offer the value engineer an opportunity to influence the design before it is turned over to production. As in the case of specification reviews, the application of value engineering techniques assures an optimum trade-off between all design parameters in the interest of reducing overall cost.

Value Engineering Task Forces. Recognizing that cost avoidance techniques are seldom completely effective, a "second look" can often produce significant savings. For this purpose VE task forces are organized to implement the VE Job Plan on specific low-value items. Each element of cost is challenged from a function/worth viewpoint and alternative approaches are developed in each case where value is considered low. Following the job plan, a proposal is generated which presents a value-engineered design for engineering management evaluation. Participation in the task force normally includes a member from Engineering, Manufacturing, and Purchasing, and a value engineering specialist.

Target Cost. For value engineering program purposes, a cost target is defined as *an attainable economic goal for the variable portion of the production cost of a specific end item at specified points in the acquisition program.* In most companies, cost targets are generated by a collaborative effort on the part of Engineering, Cost Estimating, and Value Engineering. Cost targets are based upon cost models which cumulatively express a significant portion of the total cost of a system or subsystem. Cost models can of course be expressed in either algebraic or graphic terms. Cost targets are generated by assigning dollar values to each element of a cost model.

It is worth noting that the objective of a value engineering program is stimulation of cost consciousness in all individuals who contribute to product cost. A cost target program provides a goal for the designer and a continuous assessment of cost performance against that goal.

ORGANIZATION

Organization for value engineering generally involves both line and staff functions. The staff role is primarily one of planning, coordination, assuring compliance with company policy, customer interface, etc. The line activity is mainly concerned with the actual "doing" of value engineering. As a staff function, value engineering is often found as an element of corporate Product Assurance (which may include Reliability, Quality Control,

Specifications, and Standards) or as a separate function reporting at the vice president level.

As a line function, the value engineering focal point is normally located within the engineering organization, particularly in defense industry where the value engineering emphasis is on design.

The Value Engineer. Basically, two types of personnel are involved in a value engineering program: those having prime responsibility for the design of a product, and those providing the focal point for cost reduction and cost avoidance as a full-time endeavor. One of the essential elements of a good value engineering program is the establishment of a comparatively small group of individuals whose *prime* responsibility involves value engineering actions which assure management that cost considerations are systematically factored into the decision-making process. This is the role of the professional value engineer.

In order to qualify for this role in the *engineering* organization, the individual should possess formal education in a field of engineering, plus a background of experience in manufacturing and cost analysis. In addition, a formal value engineering course (involving 40 to 80 classroom hours) plus a certain amount of on-the-job training is necessary to complete the background of education and experience essential to practice value engineering as a professional endeavor.

Within other organizational units, such as *manufacturing* and *materiel,* the qualifications are in accordance with general qualifications for employment in those areas. In the area of *procurement,* for example, it is more important that the individual be well founded in the principles of good purchasing practices than that he possess an engineering degree. Nevertheless, to perform as a *value specialist* in the areas of manufacturing and materiel, the individual should receive formal training in value engineering and on-the-job training.

In all cases, it is important that the full-time value engineer be well respected throughout his organization, possess a high degree of initiative and creativity, and, in a true sense, be *cost oriented.* The ability to sell ideas also is important to the success of the individual as well as that of the value engineering program.

6
Vendor Rating

In recent years, Vendor Rating based on price, delivery, and quality has become standard practice in hundreds of industrial purchasing departments. The "Incoming Material Rating Plan" developed by the General Electric Company has been widely quoted. Its purpose is to establish a procedure by which Quality Control and Purchasing, working together in operating departments, can more readily fulfill their objective of obtaining quality product at minimum cost. With changes in weightings to suit specific requirements, the plan is applicable in any company.

PROCEDURE

(1) Where past supplier data are available, the Quality Control Organization should compile a list of items, using drawing and part number, which are considered troublesome qualitywise.

(2) The Purchasing Organization should in like manner compile a list of items which are considered troublesome because of price or service or both.

(3) From the lists of items compiled from (1) and (2) above, agreement between Quality Control and Purchasing should result in a *single* list of items to be used in the Rating Program.

(4) (a) Where there is no past supplier information, the above data will have to be compiled from future information as it is developed, or—

    (b) A supplier's facilities check and appraisal program may be employed with this plan.

RELATIONSHIP

(1) Purchasing has the sole responsibility for the choice of supplier and placing the order.

(2) Quality Control's responsibility is to assist Purchasing by furnishing pertinent quality information on incoming materials.

(3) Purchasing will be guided by the following factors for determining a source of supply:
1. Quality.
2. Price.
3. Service.

From a survey taken at six purchasing management conferences and three quality control meetings, the following weights have been assigned.

1. Quality	=	40	Points
2. Price	=	35	,,
3. Service	=	25	,,
Total		100	,,

Note: (This plan is flexible. The above points may be varied to suit specific requirements if necessary, without changing the workings of the plan.)

EXAMPLE

Quality = 40 Points

Quality Control will base its ratings on the assumption that incoming lots are either acceptable or rejectable.

If all lots are acceptable over the period of time, such as one month, during which the item is being rated, a number of 40 will be assigned as above to Quality. Obviously, if not all lots are good or acceptable, this number 40 must be reduced according to the degree in which there are unacceptable lots. This may be done as follows:

Determine the ratio of acceptable lots received as a percentage and multiply by 40. This will give the number to be assigned to Quality. (See Exhibit I for example.)

$$Price = 35\ Points$$

Purchasing will base its price rating on the net prices as shown in Exhibit II.

Lowest price always equals full 35 points. Therefore .93 equals 35 points in this example. In order to adjust the rating for Suppliers B and C, the differential in points must be found.

$$Supplier\ B = (.93/1.16) = 80$$
$$35\ Points \times .80 = 28\ points\ for\ B$$
$$Supplier\ C = (.93/1.23) = .76$$
$$35 \times .76 = 26.6\ points\ for\ C$$

The result:

Supplier	A	B	C
Net Price	.93	1.16	1.23
Price Factor Rating	.35	.28	26.6

$$Service = 25\ Points$$

Purchasing will base its service rating on promises kept and allied conditions. This may be a straight percentage:

Supplier	A	B	C
Promises Kept, etc.	90%	95%	100%

In order to adjust the rating number 25 to represent rightfully each supplier, we may simply multiply it by the percentage of promises kept, etc. For Supplier A that would be 90% × 25 = 22.5, etc.

Supplier	A	B	C
Promises Kept	90%	95%	100%
Service Factor Rating	22.5	23.8	25

Exhibit I

Drawing and Part Number	Lots Received	Lots Accept.	Lots Rej.	% Accept.	Factor	Q.C. Rating No.
Supplier A	60	54	6	90	40	36
Supplier B	60	56	4	93.3	40	37.3
Supplier C	20	16	4	80.0	40	32.0

Note: If it is desired to rate lots closer, a system of fractional lots can be used. Thus if an unacceptable lot is only half or one-tenth bad, it could be said 0.5 or 0.1 lots were unacceptable, etc. This would distinguish between suppliers with a total lot unacceptable and only a small part of a lot unacceptable.

Exhibit II

Drawing and Part Number Supplier	A	B	C
Unit Price	1.00	1.25	1.50
Discount	.10	.15	.30
	.90	1.10	1.20
Transportation	.03	.06	.03
Net Price	.93	1.16	1.23

Exhibit III

Drawing and Part Number Supplier	A	B	C
Quality (40)	36	37.3	32
Price (35)	35	28	26.6
Service (25)	22.5	23.8	25
Total Rating	93.5	89.1	83.6

Exhibit IV

Total in Points	Excellent 100	Good 99–94	Fair 93–87	Needs Investigation Under 87
In Individual Factors	Excellent	Good	Fair	Questionable
Quality	40	39–38	37–36	Under 36
Price	35	34–33	32–31	Under 31
Service	25	24–32	22–21	Under 21

Note: As in Quality, a closer or finer evaluation of service can be used. Again, fractional lots delivered on time can be reported, so that as an example, the final percentage might be based on 11.75 lots out of 14 received on time, etc.

Composite Rating (Perfect = 100 Points)

The "total rating" now shown in Exhibit III becomes a guide to Purchasing for choosing a supplier. In order to appraise the rated factors, a factor guidance scale is shown in Exhibit IV. (This scale may also be adjusted to satisfy specific requirements).

7
Material Management

Material management is the name given to material handling functions as they pertain to the physical distribution chain.

There are, essentially, two distinct types of material handling functions in industrial operations: (1) those concerned directly with the manufacturing process, and (2) those concerned with physical distribution, i.e., the transportation, storage, inventory control, and so forth, of raw material, finished or semi-finished products, and the like.

Material handling in a manufacturing process becomes essentially a manufacturing process itself through integration into the production line. For that reason, it is almost invariably in the purview of production management and tends to become largely a matter of engineering compatibility with production machinery. In certain high-volume consumer goods industries such as food or liquor, nonproduction material handling and protective packaging functions tend to be integrated into the production processes as well, but these cases are the exception rather than the rule. And although certain types of handling equipment may be common to both production and nonproduction material handling operations—fork lift trucks and conveyors are two examples—by and large the two activities tend to be separate and distinct, both in their orientation and in their management.

An analysis of production-line material handling, therefore, belongs properly with appraisal of the manufacturing function. It is nonproduction-line material handling that is given the title material management, in that it concerns itself with the physical distribution process.

Under the material management concept, authority of material handling personnel extends to other related activities such as packaging, storage, and transportation. Further responsibilities relate to production, sales/marketing, customer relations, and other areas. The goal of material management cannot be defined independently; it must be considered in the light of its relationship to this wide range of other industrial functions.

TRADE-OFF

A pronounced shift away from the "hardware" approach to material management—i.e., the installation of specific equipment to perform a specific task—has been recognizable in recent years. In its place there has evolved a systems approach to this function, exemplified by increasing emphasis on the concept of the "trade-off."

"Trade-off" implies throughput systemization of material handling, transportation, warehousing, and protective packaging—with a marketing goal. Two fundamental questions are: "Can we render the same level of customer service at less cost?" and "Can we render a better level of customer service at no increase in cost?" In the process of answering these questions, it becomes clear, for instance, that added expense in material handling activities may be offset by even greater savings in transport costs, packaging, and storage space—and improved customer service.

Similarly, with an overview of the total movement system, it is possible to determine in what instances an increase in transport cost (by switching to premium transportation) will be justified by savings in handling, protective packaging, and warehousing.

An important factor in this trend has been the development of new containerized systems and unit loading techniques which present savings in handling, transportation, and storage. Even more important, however, are the new marketing opportunities they offer in the form of improved customer service and increased unit of sales. Recognition of this factor has led many companies to develop their movement systems—handling, packaging, containerization, transportation, etc.—to a point of maximum compatibility with their customers' receiving and production facilities. In companies with strong marketing orientation, this approach will extend to sending teams to the customer's facility to assist him in developing more efficient receiving and handling systems.

ORGANIZATION

Company executives and department heads with responsibilities in this area will vary from company to company, with a great deal depending on the departmental alignment of these three specific activities: shipping-receiving, loading-unloading, and warehousing. It is not uncommon, for instance, to have shipping-receiving under Production, loading-unloading under Traffic, and warehousing under Sales. Even further divisions will occur, as when shipping is under Traffic and receiving under Purchasing. Similarly, in the case of warehousing, one department may be responsible for locating warehouses, another for constructing and equipping them, a third for operating them, and a fourth for securing full utilization.

Although there is a definite trend toward systemization of material handling throughout these segmented activities, there is little evidence that any one individual job function is consistently *the* prime mover. Instead, material handling problems tend to be bucked up to the various department managers concerned directly and indirectly with customer service, for group action at the point where there is an overview of the total movement system.

Responsibility for Equipment. Customer-service or marketing orientation is the most reliable clue to the identity of individuals actually responsible for purchases of material handling equipment for nonproduction line use. Although the actual number of departments involved may be as few as one or as many as six or seven, the functional responsibility of an individual for some aspect of the movement system is a far more accurate indication of his activity and influence than is his specific job title.

Studies show that these individuals carry the following departments: Traffic/Transportation; Distribution; Sales; Warehousing; Production (where it includes responsibility for shipping-receiving functions); Engineering (where concerned with loading and unloading facilities); and Purchasing.

It should be noted that material handling engineers perform an important staff function, particularly in companies which produce uniform products like canned goods in large volume, and have opportunities for total integration of handling systems. However, operations of this type are relatively few in number, and since material handling engineers are in general attached to production staffs, their influence does not usually carry over very far into nonproduction handling activities.

TYPES OF MATERIAL-HANDLING EQUIPMENT

Material handling represents 35% to 40% of *all* production costs—in some basic industries, as much as 75% or even more. It is one of the few areas where costs can still be substantially reduced as shown by the fact that handling costs vary widely among plants with the same general volume of output, even in the same industry. The plant hampered by the limitations of old buildings, the plant that "just grew," the plant where material handling is regarded as not specially related to basic manufacturing, all these can often be helped to lower handling costs. However, lack of proper planning of buildings has in many cases made the task, if not impossible, at least impractical from an investment standpoint. Only when management becomes sufficiently alerted to this problem to pinpoint *actual* material handling costs and analyze their effect on other functions can their true significance in overall cost control be appreciated.

Where only warehousing operations are concerned, handling problems are usually more readily identifiable. It is in the complexity of manufacturing or processing areas that the handling factor often becomes obscured and must be isolated by careful operation analysis.

In the face of the increasing pressure on costs, the ultimate solution is of course the complete new facility. This calls for a true *integrated handling system,* based on the concept of a complete producing unit, planned with an eye on the full effect of each single function on all other functions. Production processes may even be modified to tie them in better with material handling. Actually, this kind of thinking goes even beyond the bounds of a plant facility. The scientific material handling system starts with the packaging of raw materials at the supplier's plant and ends only when the product reaches the customer's receiving dock.

The activities which comprise the *total* material handling system are many. The following list is generally accepted:
1. Packaging at vendor's plant.
2. Transportation from vendor.
3. Unloading.
4. Receiving.
5. Stores (indoors and out).
6. Issuing to production.
7. In-process handling.
8. In-process storage.
9. Workplace handling.
10. Intradepartmental handling.
11. Interdepartmental handling.
12. Intraplant handling.
13. Handling related to auxiliary functions.
14. Packaging (consumer).
15. Packaging (protective).
16. Finished goods warehousing.
17. Loading.
18. Shipping.
19. Transportation.
20. Record keeping.

Each of these areas may be studied and improved separately. Package design, for example, can have as much influence on handling methods as can more obvious factors such as floor capacities and the like. A significant increase in effective floor space can often be attained by slightly altering the dimensions or type of a shipping container. Such an approach requires an examination of raw material sources and the effect of their packaging and shipping methods on costs. At the other end, the handling costs of market distribution facilities must be considered.

"PROCESSING ON THE MOVE"

The *integrated material handling systems concept* seeks to eliminate material handling as such. The key word is "flow," that is, *processing on the move,* with coordinated flow lines extending from the raw material source, through receiving, processing, warehousing, and shipping, and ultimately to primary distribution centers.

Recent years have produced a number of outstanding examples of the effectiveness of this approach. Some are large-scale operations. But even in medium-size plants, the processing-on-the-move approach has been used with highly effective results.

The trend toward integrated handling systems is by no means confined to completely new plants. The approach has been used to modernize existing plants, at least to the extent permitted by building limitations. The highly competitive brewing industry, for example, has taken some noteworthy steps in this direction. In the most modern brewing operations, empty cans come from the supplier's plant in large, specially designed bulk bins from which they are fed by gravity directly to the filling lines. Intermediate handling has been eliminated, but this saving was made possible only by coordinating the shipping methods of the can supplier with the best system for the user.

Because an integrated handling system means lower costs, it has an important place in the planning of any new production facility. This calls for a free interchange of ideas. The architect, the industrial and process engineers, and the product designers, all must participate.

Terms like "integrated handling" and "systems concept" often conjure up a vision of highly specialized automatic equipment. This is a misconception. To be sure, strides have been made in the design of highly specialized handling equipment. But a wide variety of near-standard equipment can be fitted to a specific situation with the use of various accessories. In fact, about 400 different kinds, types, and varieties of material handling equipment are presently available. They are classified by the International Material Management Society and the American Society of Mechanical Engineers into nine major classifications as follows:

Either mobile or fixed
    1.000 conveyors
    2.000 cranes
    3.000 positioning equipment

Mobile
    4.000 industrial vehicles
    5.000 motor vehicles
    6.000 railroad cars
    7.000 marine vehicles
    8.000 air transports

Fixed
    9.000 containers and supports

There may be as many as 1,000 pieces of equipment or devices in some of these classifications. The following paragraphs describe a representative few of the devices commercially available.

Monorail systems are a highly efficient means of handling loads on an intermittent basis. The advantages are: no rigid floor requirements, better use of overhead space, and little or no need for aisle space. However, routes and areas served must be more or less fixed, and auxiliary mobile equipment may be needed to supplement the system.

Conveyors are one of the mainstays for handling material in various forms, and some innovations in the conveyor field have still further increased their versatility. In the so-called "power and free" overhead conveyor system, loads are actually suspended from the "free" overhead conveyor line and are moved along by spring-loaded pusher bars connected to a parallel overhead power chain. Use of the spring-loaded pushers permits banking or backing up of loads when desired, thus providing storage for anticipated peak requirements at the production unit, and the flexibility of varying load speeds.

In the field of roller and belt conveyors, automatic control, combined with standard conveyor equipment, has produced mass-handling systems of high capacity with the advantages of en route storage, stop-offs for processing, and automatic package sorting.

Other interesting types of conveyor equipment have been developed in recent years. Thus a flexible steel belt conveyor can be made to go around turns in snakelike fashion, eliminating the roller curves required with a conventional belt conveyor; and the oscillating trough conveyor carries bulk materials along in a uniform, continuous forward movement (even up-grade) by vibration.

Conveyors are also being used as moving assembly benches which make for better control of workers' output and simplify inventory control because materials can move more directly.

Forklift trucks have been greatly improved in versatility and maneuverability, with direct bearing on effective use of floor space. Not so long ago, a ten-foot-wide aisle was the narrowest in which a conventional 4,000-pound forklift truck could turn 90 degrees, pick up a load, and return to its original position. Innovations have reduced required aisle widths considerably in the last few years. The trend now is to look upon the basic fork truck as a power source for various attachments or devices that can be changed quickly to meet varying needs.

Out of doors, forklift trucks are becoming bigger and more stable. The trend is toward greater maneuverability, and at the same time, better balance, plus (as an outgrowth of OSHA), all-weather driver protection and a full complement of safety features in relation to both the driver and the load.

The driverless tractor and train is a development that is commercially applicable. Such a system can be used to dispatch individual loaded cars to remote points, where they are dropped and empties are picked up—all without the need for a driver-operator. Guidance and motive power for the tractor come either from a single wire hung overhead or running in an inconspicuous groove in the floor, or from a line painted on the floor that reflects light rays to light-sensitive devices within the tractor which keep it "on the beam" as it moves along its path. Overall control of the system is handled from a central programming panel where routings, stopovers, and pickups may be preselected in a few seconds.

The unit load concept is becoming standard practice. The idea is not new, but as the full potential of integrated handling has become apparent, it has taken on new meaning. Materials and products are being moved in unit loads, not only in the plant and warehouse, but over highways and railroads and by air. Unit load is based, to a great extent, on modules (sizes in multiples) which coordinate carriers, pallets, package shapes and sizes, etc., so that they square off and fit with minimum wasted space and dunnage.

The idea of a container of full trailer-truck size, separate from the rolling stock, opens up tremendous possibilities not only for lowering loading and unloading costs, but for reducing breakage and spoilage. Full trailer-size, the cargo unit can be loaded and blocked for shipment at the output end of the production line, with a free choice of transportation media. The "packaged" cargo unit may be conveyed by railroad car to a seaboard point, picked up as a unit, and loaded aboard ship for over-water shipment. Each transfer between media is performed at a fraction of the cost of manual handling. Other outstanding advantages offered by these sealed cargo units are protection against pilferage and elimination of special export packing.

Modern pallet handling equipment has helped greatly to sell the "unit load" idea. Plant-wide pallet systems now include automatic stackers (palletizers), unstackers for depalletizing incoming loads, pallet conveyors, and automatic fast-acting floor-to-floor pallet elevators. The automatic pallet loaders available today can take many different packages from production lines, sort and stack them in any desired sequence, and forward the loaded pallet by conveyor to warehouse or shipping dock—all without manual effort. Systems like this can save as much as 90% of the cost of manual stacking.

Here again, the integrated handling system concept comes in.

When all loading and unloading were done manually, the type of truck or railroad car was of minor consequence. The only requirement was manual labor—and plenty of it. For pallet handling, however, highway truck bodies must be suitable for handling pallet loads.

Pallet manufacturers are trying to develop standard pallet sizes, but the multiplicity of package sizes makes this difficult. Meanwhile, the concept of unit loading without pallets is growing. This can be accomplished by using a fork truck clamping arrangement for gripping and moving the assembled stack as a unit.

AUTOMATION CONCEPTS

Computers are increasingly being used to control various aspects of material handling. Some of the computerized material handling systems do a remarkably complete job. In one plant, large component parts are placed on pallets on a conveyor. The computer then directs the movement of each pallet to an empty storage rack in a warehouse (unlighted because machines do not need to see). As a pallet is deposited in the storage rack, the computer notes its exact location. Later on, when the part on the pallet is needed for assembly or further processing, the computer brings it out of storage on command. Other automation concepts and components include ultrasonic or light-interrupted readers for filling containers to preset levels, photoelectric cells and read-color or other graphic codes for dispatching mixed loads on containers, and the like.

PLANNING, PRE-PLANNING, AND ORGANIZATION

An obvious corollary to the integration of material handling with plant design is the integration of the building and the handling system with all other related functions—for example, the production process and related equipment. Material handling, however, is a primary function, and in many situations, is almost as important to the success of an enterprise as the production process. It calls for extensive preplanning when new building construction is being considered. Preplanning, in this case, means that before actually planning a new plant or any sizable plant expansion, management must decide who will participate in the actual planning, and what factors are to be considered. At the preplanning stage, capital limitations are assessed, a team is chosen, and goals are established. The actual planning of technical and other aspects should proceed only after this groundwork has been laid.

The integration of the material handling function with other parts of the modern industrial enterprise is no easy task. Experiences in recent years have dramatized the importance of material handling, and many companies have adopted the materials manager type of organization.

Education work has been going forward, with traveling clinics and related activities sponsored by the Material Handling Institute and the American Material Handling Society.

8
Inventory Management

Approximately one third of America's industrial capitalization is in inventory, and yet industry clings to traditional rules of thumb to control this investment, such as the rule of "turnover." When sales go up, most managements permit inventories to become inflated; when sales go down, they stress inventory reduction. The only policy directive given to inventory managers in many companies is simply, "Keep your inventory down but don't run out of stock."

It is the purpose of this chapter to acquaint managers with some of the newer, scientific methods of inventory control. Certainly, there is still much to be done in the study of the means for evaluating and controlling inventories, but the methods to be discussed here are well tested and tried and have proven their value. However, no formula is a substitute for judgment, and it is well to remember that the following approaches are offered as guides only.

SCIENTIFIC INVENTORY CONTROL

The inventory manager must make two decisions as he runs his inventory. To begin with, he has a dwindling supply of stock on hand: He must decide *when* to replenish or reorder his stock.

INVENTORY MANAGEMENT

Secondly, he must decide *how much* to order. These two decisions, *when* and *how much* determine the size of his inventory, and are illustrated in Exhibit I.

In Exhibit I we start with a given stock position on January 1, and gradually the stock drops lower and lower until, finally, we must reorder or face a stock-out. This is the *reorder point*. The determination of the recorder point determines the *cushion*.

The Cushion. Every inventory has a cushion. The average checking account for example, probably has no less than three cushions. Few people reduce their account to zero for fear of error in the figures. This gives one cushion, or "protective stock." Secondly, there is a two to three-day period from the time a check is written until it is deducted from the account. This delay provides a second cushion. Thirdly, many people put $25 in their account but do not record it in their balance. This $25 represents a third, or "safety" cushion.

Cushion or safety stock arises in industrial inventory from the fear of overdrawing or stocking out.

It is apparent from Exhibit I that if we use an average of six

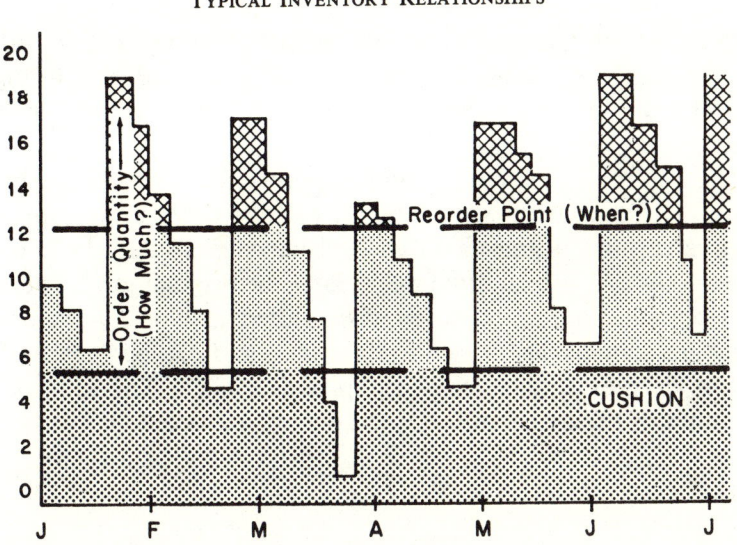

EXHIBIT I
TYPICAL INVENTORY RELATIONSHIPS

units every two weeks (the normal length of time to get this particular item), then we dare not wait until stocks get down to six units to reorder. If we did, we would find ourselves overdrawn or out of stock *half the time,* since it probably would be just as likely as not that goods would move faster or more slowly than anticipated during the time between reorder and actual receipt of new supplies. Hence, as a matter of protection, we must reorder sooner. The question of just when to reorder will be discussed in detail later. Suffice to say here, that the problem of *when* is the problem of delivery. The more effectively we control our reorder point, the better we control our stock-outs, and, hence, our ability to deliver when needed.

The question of *how much* is an economic problem. In Exhibit I, we ordered twelve units at a time. We could have ordered one at a time (more frequently of course). Or we could have ordered 100 at a time (less frequently). The question of how much to order is a question of economic order quantities.

Space will not permit a fully detailed discussion of economic order quantities or reorder points, but we can explore them to provide an understanding of their meaning and use.[1]

ECONOMIC ORDER QUANTITIES

Two factors or variables affect the decision of how much to order. In any company, these factors are clearly defined and brought into sharp conflict on the one side by the foreman and on the other by the controller.

The foreman sees before him on every machine the costs of setup. He sees numerous examples of jobs that are set up, and then set up again and again each year. A setup may be broken down for a new job and two weeks later the original job is back on the machine. To him, setups represent losses in capacity and costs. They are actually controlled in the office and can be increased at will by decreasing the size of the production lot. The solution in the mind of the foreman is to plan better: to make long runs—for

---

An early detailed approach is given in the book by the author of the *Encyclopedia of Management* entry on which this chapter is based: Reinfeld, Nyles V., "Production Control," Englewood Cliffs, N.J., 1959.

INVENTORY MANAGEMENT 63

example, to run a year's supply at a time and thus pay for only one setup a year.

This cost of setup is the *cost of getting*. (Where items are purchased, it is the cost of going through the motions of procurement.) The cost of getting is actually a whole family of costs, and can be more precisely defined as follows: The *costs of getting* are those costs that we pay for twice when we produce an order in two lots instead of one. Upon reflection, we can see by this definition that many costs are increased when we produce two small lots instead of one larger one: the setup costs of the foreman; expediting, scheduling and paperwork costs; some inspection and scrap costs; and so on. In sum, from the shop's point of view an economic run is to make a long run—possibly a year's supply.

In the office, the controller must meet increasing demands for money. Methods improvements cost money and pay off later. New machinery may pay a high return but it takes years to recover the investment. Better plant and facilities, pay raises, increased expenditures on advertising, sales, marketing, larger payrolls, more research and staff positions, all require funds. The controller wants to get money *from* inventory, not put more money *in* it! Inventory not only drains off money, but also costs money to store it. These are the *costs of having*—the inventory carrying charges.

The carrying charges include the following: interest on money, taxes, insurances, storage space, clerical and physical inventorying, deterioration, and obsolescence. There are, in fact, over 200 items that can be listed in the cost of carrying inventory. These factors can be computed as a percent of the average inventory. For example, a 25% cost of having could mean that a $1,000,000 inventory costs $250,000 per year to carry.

In recent years, the industrial average cost of having has increased from about 18% to about 25%. This increase may reflect a reinterpretation of the interest figure: 6% at one time for a common figure. Today, many companies use return on investment (for example, 15%).

These two variables, the costs of getting and the costs of having, determine the economic order quantity. Note that the annual costs of getting go down as the variable portion of inventory goes up, since larger order quantities mean fewer orders per year. The

64 VNR CONCISE GUIDE TO BUSINESS LOGISTICS

Exhibit II
Costs of Variable Portion* of Inventory of a Valve Body

	Order Quantity in Months' Usage					
	1	2	3	6	12	
			Costs			
A. Annual Cost of Getting	$192	$96	$64	$32	$16	($16 × frequency of ordering per year)
Average Variable Inventory	$128	$256	$384	$768	$1536	(½ of amount put into inventory)
B. Annual Cost of Having	$21	$43	$64	$128	$256	(17% of average inventory)
Total Cost		$213	$139	$128	$160	$272

"Givens" on Valve Body
Cost of Getting—$16
Cost of Having—17%
Monthly Usage—$256

* These are the costs over and above the cost of carrying the cushion, or safety stocks.

carrying charges, however, go up as average inventory increases. These relationships are illustrated in the cost analysis table, Exhibit II.

The lowest total cost in this example occurs when we order three months' supply of the item. At that time, our costs are $128. Note, that although the costs go up as we deviate from the economic order quantity (three months), they increase less rapidly when we over-order than when we under-order. Hence, it is better to err on the high side than the low side.

If the data in the table are plotted, they become a curve as shown in Exhibit III. The data can be generalized to develop a formula as follows: using G for cost of getting, M for monthly usage in dollars, H for cost of having, and EOQ for economic order quantity in months' usage, we get:

$$\text{A. Annual Cost of Getting} = \frac{12G}{EOQ}$$

$$\text{B. Annual Cost of Having} = \frac{(M \times EOQ \times H)}{2}$$

Solving for minimum total cost, i.e., finding the trough or bottom point of the total cost curve A + B, by setting its derivative (a mathematical operation) equal to zero and solving for EOQ, we get:

$$EOQ = \sqrt{\frac{G}{M} \times \frac{24}{H}}.$$

This is the formula for economic order quantities in months.

EXHIBIT III
TOTAL INVENTORY COST VS. ORDER QUANTITY

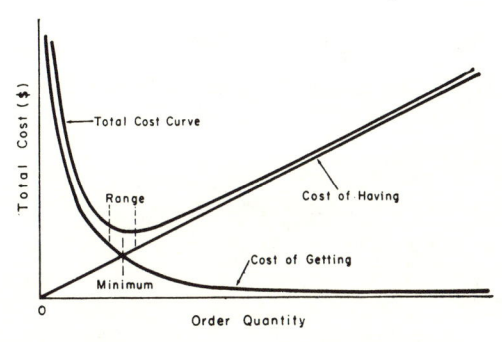

Using the data of the previous example, we get:

$$EOQ = \sqrt{\frac{16}{256} \times \frac{24}{\frac{1}{6}}} = 3.$$

This is the classic Economic Lot Formula. Numerous variations of it will be found in the literature. For example, by slight changes in the components, it is possible to get the answer in terms of dollars, weeks, periods, pieces, and so on. It is often given in terms of units, rather than months' supply, viz.:

$$EOQ \text{ (pieces)} = \sqrt{\frac{2U(S + O)}{HC}}$$

66 VNR CONCISE GUIDE TO BUSINESS LOGISTICS

Here U is usage in pieces per year, C is the cost per piece, H is the cost of having, or carrying charges, per year, expressed as a percentage, and the expression (S + O) is the getting costs in terms of "set up and order" costs.

For purchased items, the same formula is used as for manufac-

EXHIBIT IV
ECONOMIC ORDER QUANTITY CHART
TO USE CHART:

Lay a straight-edge on the two outer variables, and read order quantity where straight-edge intersects inner scale.

COMPUTATION OF CARRYING CHARGES
(Yearly Cost Charged Against Value of Inventory)

Interest Rate on Investment _____%

$$\text{Insurance Rate} = \frac{\text{Insurance Cost} \times 100}{\text{Ave. Inventory (\$)}}$$ _____%

$$\text{Storage Rate} = \frac{\text{All Storage Costs} \times 100}{\text{Ave. Inventory (\$)}}$$ _____%

$$\text{Obsolescence Rate} = \frac{\text{Obsolescence Losses (\$)} \times 100}{\text{Ave. Inventory (\$)}}$$ _____%

$$\text{Deterioration Rate} = \frac{\text{Deterioration Costs} \times 100}{\text{Ave. Inventory (\$)}}$$ _____%

Taxes, Miscellaneous _____%

Total Yearly Carrying Charge _____%

CONVERSION TO YOUR OWN CARRYING CHARGE

To convert chart to your own yearly carrying charge, multiply figures on 24% side of vertical line by conversion factor, determined by following formula:

$$\text{Conversion Factor} = \sqrt{\frac{24}{\text{Your Yearly Carrying Charge (\%)}}}$$

EXHIBIT IV

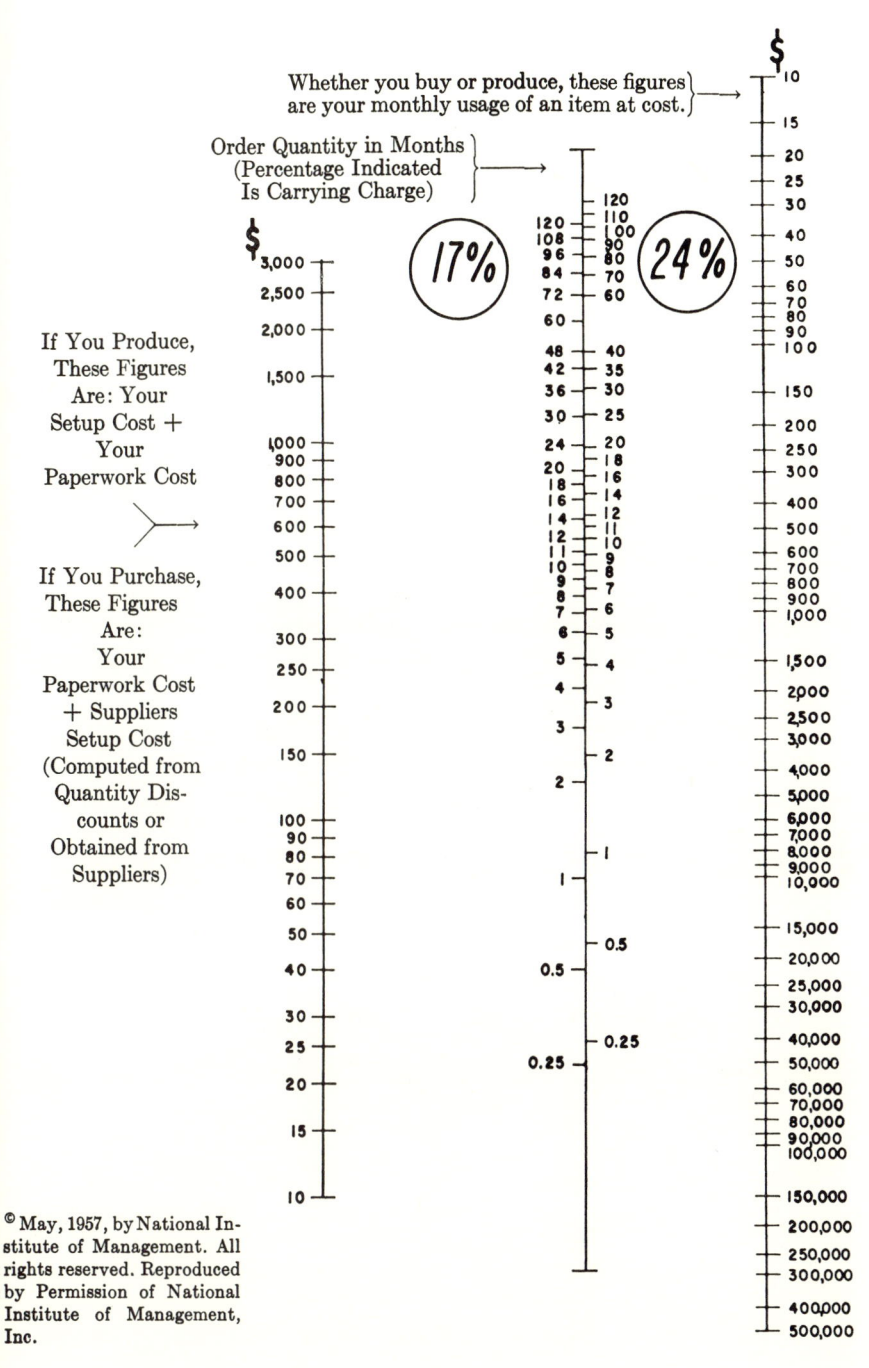

tured items, but the S in the expression (S + O) drops out, since there is no set-up cost, and the O becomes the cost of processing the order (such as paperwork, cost of receiving, etc.).

It can be seen from Exhibit III, without resort to calculus, that the optimum order quantity occurs at the point where the linearly rising carrying charges cross the decreasing curve of procurement or "getting" costs—i.e., where the annual carrying cost equals the annual cost of getting.

The formula is cumbersome in practice, despite its relative simplicity, since it does require numerous calculations. For this reason, it is usually best to reduce the formula to a slide rule or graphic solution as illustrated in Exhibit IV.

Using the original example again, with a $16 cost of getting, $256 monthly usage and 17% cost of having, we read from the chart an EOQ of three months. The chart offers great flexibility, permitting a wide selection of costs and usages in determining the EOQ. For example, a $10 cost of getting, $10 monthly usage, at 17%, gives us an EOQ of twelve months, whereas, a $10 cost of getting, a $1,000 monthly usage, at 17%, gives an EOQ of 1.2 months.

Obviously it does make a difference whether we order 1.2 months' supply or a year's supply at a time. In fact, it makes a very great difference as is illustrated by the comparison in Exhibit V.

By means of the formula (or chart) it is almost always possible

EXHIBIT V
COST EFFECT OF DEPARTING FROM ECONOMIC ORDER QUANTITY

If you produce (or buy) only this part of the proper order quantity	Then your base costs will increase by this amount
10%	405%
20%	160%
33%	67%
50%	25%
80%	3%
100%	0%
125%	3%
200%	25%
300%	67%
500%	160%
1000%	405%

to keep our base costs within 3% of the optimum. This is true despite great errors that are inherent in the rough data that must go into the formula. For example, it is not uncommon to encounter wide variations of thinking relative to carrying charges. In the same company, depending on the interpretation of the basic data in the carrying charges, one individual may favor 17% while another favors 24%. The lack of agreement loses significance when we compare one view against the other in the chart. At 24%, the EOQ becomes 2.6 months compared to three months at 17%. This is a variation of about 12% and is well within the "ball-park area" of a 3% base cost increase.

It will also be found that wide ranges of errors are possible in the forecast with similar results. For example, if we had used $384 instead of $256 as the monthly usage in the original example, our order quantity would become (from the chart) about 2.5 months. This is certainly an acceptable error according to our ball park analysis, and such deviations in forecasts are common.

How well could we do without the formula in estimating the proper order quantity? The chances of good results would be slim. For any company stressing turnover as the basis for running an inventory the chances favor great errors. Thus, an attempt to order everything four times a year (not uncommon in industry) would result in the correct EOQ in our original example, but would produce only ¼ of the EOQ in the second example just cited, and would order 3.33 times the correct amount in the third example.

The only conclusion that can be reached is that even though we are not able to forecast precisely, or estimate our costs of having or getting, we are nevertheless much safer with the formula than hunch. *The formula will almost always put us within 3% of the base cost.* Hunch may, but usually will not. Studies by the present writer, using actual company cost data, forecasts, and usage figures, where order quantities have been selected without formula, have revealed order quantities ranging from one piece all the way up to 100, on the same item.

THE "ABC" ANALYSIS

The EOQ formula is applicable to in-process stores as well as to finished goods. (For purchased items, separate computations are required for quantity discounts, to see whether buying the larger quantity would save more than would be involved in carrying the additional inventory.) However, applying a formula to a company with thousands upon thousands of items, even when the formula is reduced to a chart or a computer is used, is a time-consuming task, and a simplifying set of rules must be developed.

If we take an inventory, forecast the annual usage of each item, and convert this to total dollar usage per item, we can then list the items in descending order, with the biggest seller at the top. The top 20% of this listing will usually cover about 80% of the total dollars involved. If we control this 20%, we control most of the dollars. These items must therefore be controlled tightly. The bottom 60% of the items in the listing will usually account for only about 10% of the dollars. Minimum control here will lower operating costs while sacrificing little by way of excess inventory costs. This method of trisecting an inventory is frequently referred to as the "ABC" method of inventory control.

Returning to the EOQ formula, we can spotcheck a few C items. If these C items end up with EOQs in excess of 12 months, the rule then becomes to order all C items annually. (Most companies place a ceiling on orders that exceed a year's supply.) Checking a few C items (using the formula sparingly) reduces the whole C category to a sound set of rules which do not violate the principles discussed. In addition, it is frequently more expensive to gather facts on costs of getting for C items than the expected savings. Hence, indirectly, the classification procedure actually saves money two ways.

Applying the formula to the A and B group involves only 40% of the work had we applied it to the whole inventory.

REORDER POINTS

The preceding discussion determined *how much* to order. We still face the question of *when*—the question of delivery.

Studies begun in 1923 at the Bell Telephone Laboratories under the direction of R. H. Wilson show that inventories tend to follow the so-called "Poisson distribution." In other words, their random fluctuations are definable by probability.

When an item is on order, there are three things that vary, creating the total fluctuations in usage: first, the length of the lead time varies. Lead times which average two weeks, may frequently vary, in practice, from one to four weeks. In a typical study made of one vendor over a period of one year involving 67 orders, the vendor took an average of 61.2 days to give delivery. *He was promising delivery in three weeks!* Secondly, the size of the orders will vary. One customer buys two pieces, another 300. Thirdly, the number of orders varies. One week we may have ten customers, another thirty.

Because the true inventory usage has three variables, it involves a so-called "tri-variate Poisson distribution." Because of the cost of solving such a formula, practice dictates simplification to something more workable. In a commonly used procedure where these advanced techniques are applied, the length of the lead time is averaged; the size of the order is averaged; and the Poisson is applied only to the number of orders. Test and comparisons between the two procedures shows that the simplified approach is practical and reasonable. This simplified procedure will be discussed here.

Exhibit I showed an item in which the usage is about twelve per month. For a two week lead time (*average*), we would expect to use about six units. However, we would not wait until we reached six units in inventory before reordering. If we did, we would stock-out half the time. By means of the Poisson formula, we can predict our chances of stock-outs for *any* given reorder point.

Or to invert the thinking, we can use the Poisson to establish the reorder point, if we will state *how many stock-outs we will accept*.

POLICY ON STOCK-OUTS

If we do not stock-out, we are carrying too much. For example, a study by R. H. Wilson at the Bell Telephone Laboratories revealed requirements as shown in Exhibit VI.

The "never" is in quotes, because theoretically, at least, there is always some slight chance of stock-outs even with a very large inventory. Note that the $200,000 increase in inventory is really an

> EXHIBIT VI
> INVENTORY REQUIREMENTS AS AFFECTED
> BY ACCEPTABLE STOCK-OUTS
>
> Accepting 1 stock-out a year required an inventory of only $76,000
>
> Accepting 1 stock-out every 2 years increased the required inventory to $100,000
>
> Accepting 1 stock-out every 5 years increased the required inventory to $134,000
>
> Accepting 1 stock-out every 10 years increased the required inventory to $167,000
>
> "Never" out of stock increased the required inventory to $276,000

increase in cushion or protective stocks. The cost of carrying such protective inventory at 25% would be $50,000 a year!

It is clear that the real decision to be made is a policy decision on stock-outs. Naturally, this policy will vary with companies and products. A common policy is to permit stock-out once every two years on all items except highly critical ones. Critical items may call for a "never" policy and hence should be carefully selected. In other words, cars can be delivered without a fifth tire, but without engines.

In the following discussion, we shall assume a policy of once every two years.

THE RELATION BETWEEN EOQ AND POLICY

For EOQ of three months' usage, there are four times a year in which a stock-out can occur (i.e., such an item will be on order four times a year). Hence, if this item stocked-out 25% of the time, it would stock-out once a year. To stock-out once every two years, would be to stock-out 12.5% of the time.

With a one-month EOQ, we could permit stock-outs only 4% of the time, to achieve a stock-out every two years.

The Poisson Solution. The formula for the Poisson is:

$$P[c] = (a^c e^{-a})/c!.$$

By this formula, we can compute the probability of using c units, when our *average* usage is a. Fortunately, we do not have to solve such a formula to get the reorder point, but can read directly from a chart, as shown in Exhibit VII.

The top of the chart gives the per cent of stock-outs we will accept. For a one-month EOQ, this was found to be 4%, if we permit one stock-out every two years. From the left, we read our usage during the lead time. Let us assume a usage of six during the lead time, such as does occur in Exhibit I.

Coming down from the top of the chart and in from the side, lines drawn from the 4% and the figure 6 meet at the (interpolated) curve reading about 11. This is the reorder point.

Cost of Stock-Out. A further extension of the Poisson may be made by using cost figures in place of company policy to get the percentage figure at the top of Exhibit VII. This approach is possible if we can develop figures showing how much it costs to stock-out. In some cases, for example, it costs very little to run across the street to buy an item. The formula for the proper per cent of stock-outs when we know the cost, is

$$\% = \frac{100 \times \text{EOQ} \times H \times C}{12 \times M \times K}$$

Where the EOQ is in dollars, H is cost of having in per cent, C is cost per piece in dollars, M is monthly usage in dollars, and K is cost of stock-out in dollars.

Example: EOQ = $308
H = 25%
C = $22
M = $308
K = $14

$$\frac{100 \times 308 \times \frac{1}{4} \times 22}{12 \times 308 \times 14} = 3.3\%$$

Hence, 3.3% would be the figure to read from the top of Exhibit VII.

Exhibit VII

REORDER POINT CHART

TO USE CHART:

1. Select correct usage figure for item to be protected.
2. Select percent of stock-outs you will accept.
3. Find point where 1 and 2 intersect: Read reorder point from curves at intersection.

IF GREATER ACCURACY IS DEMANDED, or where usage during lead time exceeds the chart, the reorder point can also be calculated directly as follows:

1. Determine "Factor" from table below based on percent of time you will accept stock-outs.
2. Take the square-root of the usage during the lead time. (This can be gotten from a table of square-roots.)
3. Multiply square-root of usage by "Factor."
4. Add usage during lead time to product found in 3.
5. Answer is the reorder point.

74

Exhibit VII (*continued*)

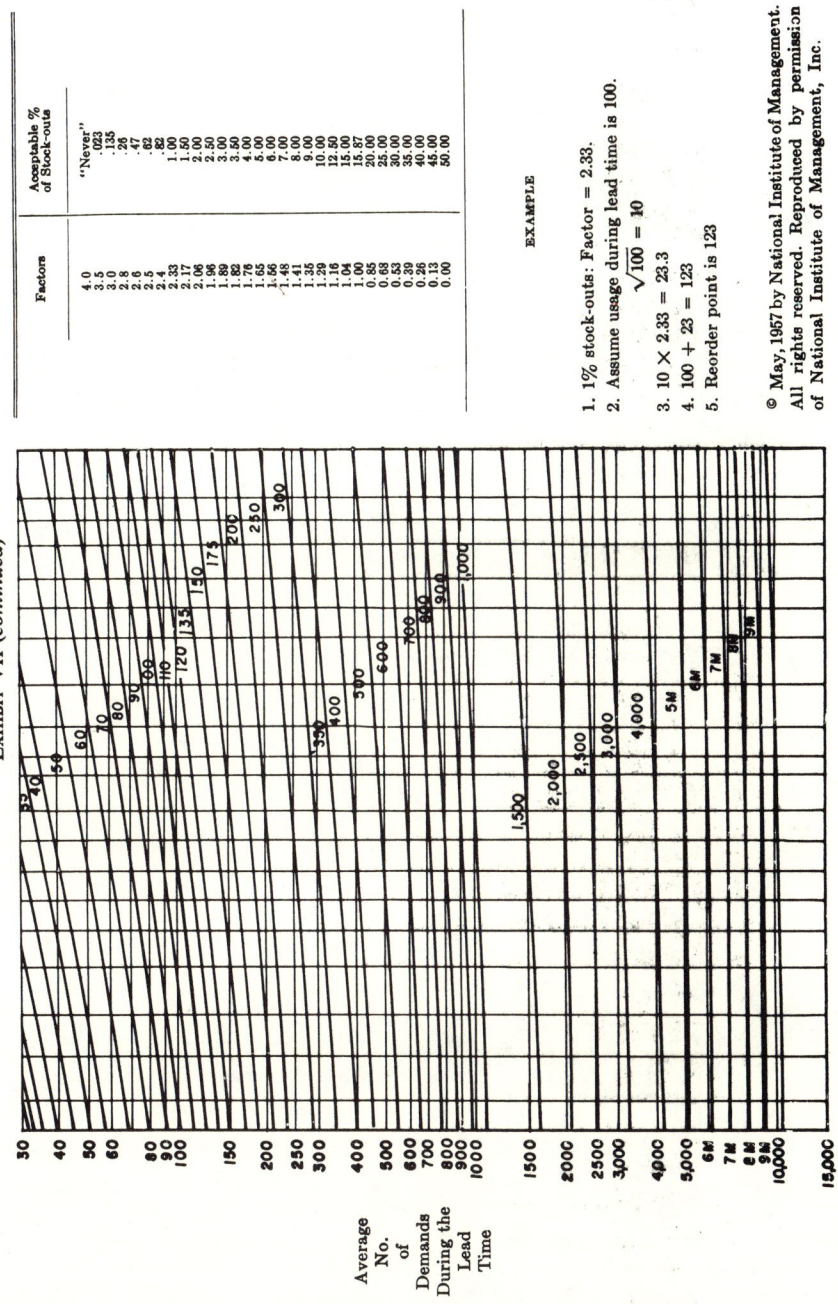

Factors	Acceptable % of Stock-outs
4.0	"Never"
3.5	.023
3.0	.135
2.8	.26
2.6	.47
2.5	.62
2.4	.82
2.33	1.00
2.17	1.50
2.06	2.00
1.96	2.50
1.89	3.00
1.82	3.50
1.76	4.00
1.65	5.00
1.56	6.00
1.48	7.00
1.41	8.00
1.35	9.00
1.29	10.00
1.16	12.80
1.04	15.87
1.00	20.00
0.85	25.00
0.68	30.00
0.53	35.00
0.39	40.00
0.26	45.00
0.13	50.00
0.00	

EXAMPLE

1. 1% stock-outs: Factor = 2.33.
2. Assume usage during lead time is 100.
3. $\sqrt{100} = 10$
4. $10 \times 2.33 = 23.3$
5. $100 + 23 = 123$
6. Reorder point is 123

© May, 1957 by National Institute of Management. All rights reserved. Reproduced by permission of National Institute of Management, Inc.

Average No. of Demands During the Lead Time

CONCLUSION

There is still much work to be done in the field of inventory control. There is need for research and greater interest on the part of industry. However, the methods described in the foregoing are in general use where advanced practice is followed. Scientific management of inventory can free significant capital for use elsewhere in the business. The two keys are economic order quantities for the variable portion of inventory, and a policy of cushions or safety stocks based on the application of mathematical probability, so that an exorbitant price will not be paid for an unnecessarily low (or "never") acceptable stockout percentage.

9
Physical Distribution Management

Physical distribution management is one of the "systems" disciplines of management wherein two or more functionally related, but previously unaffiliated, areas are conjoined to form a cohesive and unitized whole.

In its broadest sense, physical distribution management is concerned with the progress of a commodity from its point of initial production to its point of ultimate consumption. Between these two extremes there may lie several intervening stages of manufacture, processing, storage, etc.; these are not properly breaks in the physical distribution chain, but are interwoven in it, either through absorption or interdisciplinary coordination.

The nucleus around which physical distribution has evolved is transportation. Until quite recently, transportation was considered a discipline in and of itself. Gradually, however, there came a realization that transportation directly affected, and was affected by, many other functions of business managment. As the "systems approach" to business management generally won favor, these functions became ever more closely associated with transportation, until the need for a new appellation—physical distribution—became apparent.

As presently conceived, physical distribution management embraces not only transportation (and its alter ego, traffic), but such other fields as material handling, material management, packaging, industrial site location, warehousing, inventory control, and order processing. It also overlaps into certain portions of the production and marketing/sales, areas. Ideally, physical distribution engineers conceive of the management of a product-oriented company as divided into three basic functional areas—production, sales, and physical distribution—all with somewhat indistinct borders relative to one another, and among them encompassing all of the firm's business activities.

This ideal is seldom realized in practice, however. The business community in general has adopted the concept of physical distribution to the extent of recognizing the interrelationship of its various components; but those components nevertheless usually continue to receive separate treatment in the organizational hierarchy. The reason is one of simple pragmatism: Sudden infusion of the physical distribution entity into a company traditionally oriented along more separatist lines could easily lead to contraproductive confusion—especially since, as a relatively new art (or science, according to one's preference), physical distribution's constraints are still too hazily defined to permit their ready application to particular situations.

It is probable that, with the passage of time, the trend will be increasingly toward implementation of some form of physical distribution management in most types of business. As the new concept's parameters are more clearly defined through academic development and practical experience, this will become structurally and operationally more feasible. Indeed, to a substantial degree, this has proven to be the case during the last decade or so. Meanwhile, physical distribution management in practice will still continue to stand for coordination of the several areas that make up its totality, without, in many cases, their organizational unification within the corporate structure.

I—TRAFFIC MANAGEMENT

Traffic management concerns itself with the totality of the transportation that is required by a company during the course of its business activities. An indication of the importance of this function may be gleaned from the fact that over 20% of the U.S. gross national product is annually spent on transportation.

Traffic management is primarily cost-oriented. This is not to demean the importance of the service factor, pertaining to such questions as promptness, reliability, consistency, etc. However, the principal job of the industrial traffic manager is cost control—a job that steadily increases in importance as a result of the inflationary trend in transportation as well as other costs.

THE TRAFFIC MANAGER

The traffic manager is normally responsible for both proprietary and purchased transportation services. With respect to the former, he must oversee administration of the company's private trucking operation (if any), as well as utilization of any private railroad cars it may own or lease. With respect to the latter, he must involve himself in such matters as negotiation of rates with for-hire carriers of all modes, handling of loss-and-damage claims, litigation before state and Federal transport regulatory agencies, the conduct of rate research, the selection of carriers and routes, etc.

In addition to these line functions, the traffic manager also has certain duties in a staff capacity. Foremost among them is formulation of the company's transportation policy, which must set forth the company's basic approach to its procurement of transportation services. Besides setting forth the criteria which will determine the company's stand on its rate, route, and service relationships with for-hire carriers (including the circumstances under which it will seek governmental regulatory intervention), such a policy will spell out the basic criteria for determining division of the company's traffic among potential modes of carriage. The fundamental question of whether a company will use common or private carriage, for example, will be an integral part of such a policy.

Further staff functions include the conduct of, or at least participation in, site location studies involving coordination with the purchasing, production, and marketing departments to select the most advantageous geographic areas (from a transportation standpoint) for the conduct of company activities, determination of the most desirable units of purchase and sales as related to transportation constraints, etc. The pervasiveness of transportation throughout the operations of most industrial concerns means that the industrial traffic manager should be consulted with regard to virtually every important business decision made by the company.

The traffic manager will also have at least some voice—and often full managerial control—in such areas as warehousing, material management, material handling, protective packaging, inventory control, order processing, and other related fields. In the most sophisticated administrative structures, all of these disciplines, in addition to the traffic management function itself, are brought together under the generic term, *physical distribution management*. However, the concept of physical distribution managment is relatively new to the business world, and many companies continue to function without this added hierarchical layer. In any event, the increased breadth of responsibility allocated to the traffic manager often gives him the authority, if not the title, of physical distribution manager.

The traffic manager's duties with regard to the company's personnel must not be overlooked. He is usually in charge of arrangements concerning the transfer of company personnel from one location to another, including the formulation of expense reimbursement policies. Business travel arrangements will also commonly be made by the traffic department, which in some cases also reviews travel expense accounts of personnel traveling on company business.

FREIGHT TRANSPORTATION

The main part of traffic management concerns itself with freight transportation. In this regard, the highly specialized nature of transportation rate structures, routing and service arrangements, governmental regulation, etc., makes centralized planning mandatory for efficient management. This means that a relatively few individuals will exercise basic company-wide control over its transportation activities.

An important management tool in this effort is the traffic manual—what amounts to a "routing guide" to be used by lower-echelon employees in the traffic department and by employees in other departments who must involve themselves in purchasing transportation services. Such a manual is a particularized extension of the transportation policy; whereas the policy specifies the ends to be achieved, the manual discusses specific means of accomplishing those ends.

Routing guides often give the names of specific carriers that must be used for the various types of transportation in which the company engages, and are highly detailed and restrictive in their application. They are also under almost continuous review because of fluctuations in the company's transportation needs and the availability of service to fulfill those needs.

Traffic department review of all invoices for transportation services is the way management ensures adherence to the standards set forth in the policy and the manual. This will not amount to a full-fledged audit—the traffic department will not normally be equipped to handle such an audit—but will be limited to a check to make certain the standardized instructions have been followed. The traffic department will also normally have charge of certifying freight bills for payment, and this requires institution of and adherence to basic control procedures.

Computer applications have in recent years helped to extend the scope of the traffic department's control over the company's transportation. Punch-card and computer printouts and other automated systems have in some companies more or less supplanted the traffic manual as a management tool, furnishing full rate, routing, and service data on a "real-time" basis. Indeed, the potential of computerization in this field is enormous and still largely untapped. Of recent note are highly sophisticated vehicle- and shipment-location systems developed independently by a number of sources, as well as software advances that permit computerized modeling of the company's entire transportation program to facilitate cost optimization. Progress in this area continues rapidly, but to date has been somewhat limited because of the inability of programmers and present-generation hardware to handle full transportation rate computerization. The disorganized for-hire transportation rate structure continues to defy efforts at full-scale computerization—a necessary step to the advent of full automation in traffic management.

It is worth noting that only the most myopic of traffic departments will restrict its activities solely to transportation services which are paid for directly by the company. Whether or not they are identified separately as such, transportation charges will be included in the price of every item purchased by the company f.o.b. its own plants. It behooves the traffic department to oversee, and if necessary assume control of, transportation arrangements on these shipments as well if it is to avoid deleterious cost effects.

An example cited by the Aerospace Industries Association is an aerospace firm which in one year purchased more than $92 million worth of goods and services from some 4,800 small business firms. The same company placed over 200,000 individual contracts—about three-quarters of its subcontracts—with small business firms employing fewer than 500 persons. In the majority of cases, these small subcontractors were without expert traffic personnel, and proper cost-control procedure in this situation virtually required management of the traffic function by the prime contractor, which alone had the capability to do so in optimum fashion.

ORGANIZATION OF THE INDUSTRIAL TRAFFIC DEPARTMENT

The traffic department of a major industrial firm may have as many as 60 to 75 employees, and may follow one of several organizational patterns. Generally, the traffic department will have two major divisions, one designated "Services," the other "Rates and Research." On occasion, there will be a third section for warehousing and a fourth for personnel administration, and an Export Traffic Manager if circumstances warrant. Exhibit I depicts such a traffic department.

PHYSICAL DISTRIBUTION MANAGEMENT 83

Exhibit I
Traffic Management Organization

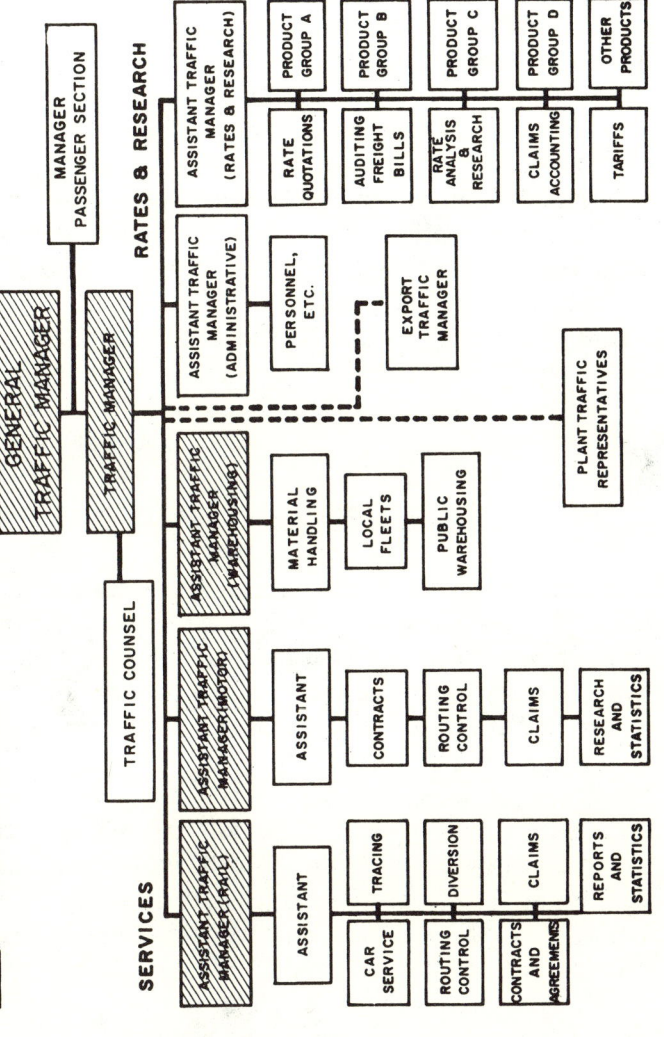

The General Traffic Manager (or Vice President—Traffic, as is often the case) is the operating head of the department, with principal operating authority delegated to the Traffic Manager and the various Assistant Traffic Managers in line functions.

There is little consistency among companies as to where the General Traffic Manager reports. If he is of vice presidential rank—and often where he is not—he usually reports to the president or a senior vice president. In other companies he reports to a vice president of manufacturing, purchasing, or finance.

Although the background of industrial traffic executives varies, the largest proportion worked their way up from clerical positions as rate clerk or tariff clerk, receiving specialized training at one of the various traffic management colleges or academies in major metropolitan areas. In the larger companies, it is a general policy to send junior traffic employees to these schools at company expense; where there are executive development programs within traffic departments, the policy is to hire college graduates and then send them to the specialized traffic schools.

OTHER DEPARTMENTS

It has been noted that the management of transportation is almost exclusively in the province of the industrial traffic manager and his chief assistants, but there are a few exceptions. These are primarily cases where the nature of the product and its method of sale are tied closely to the type of transportation and the specific transport equipment used.

An example would be bulk chemicals, where very often the customer's receiving and production facilities will have a considerable bearing on how the product is shipped. Since the producer's own production, storage, and handling facilities would also be involved, these personnel would become involved in transportation decisions: traffic manager; sales manager; plant or production manager; material handling engineer or plant engineer; warehouse manager; and packaging engineer.

On inbound shipments of raw materials, the alignment would be similar, with the purchasing agent replacing the sales manager. The traffic manager would still be the prime mover in this group, however, inasmuch as the actual transportation cost is usually

50% or more of the total costs in the procurement or distribution operation. Cases of this type will usually involve bulk commodities or large volume shipments of uniform goods.

TRANSPORTATION MANAGEMENT IN SMALLER COMPANIES

There is a marked difference between the larger companies and the smaller companies in transportation-buying practices. The larger companies—about 4,000 or so in number—have highly organized traffic departments and strict rules of procedure, and in this respect there is very little difference between one company and another. In smaller companies, however, the transportation management function is seldom formally organized, with the result that the "principal influence" (if there is one) may be anybody from the shipping clerk to the office manager or even the company president himself.

It has already been noted that many of these smaller companies handle routing and carrier selection in accordance with specific instructions furnished them by traffic departments of larger companies to whom they sell. The use of automation for purchase order-writing by these larger companies almost always encompasses automatic print-out on the purchase order of pre-programmed shipping instructions to the supplier. In one not abnormal case, the general traffic department of a major retail chain furnishes such shipping instructions to some 4,000 vendors and will not accept merchandise shipped otherwise.

Similarly, these smaller companies will usually have their inbound shipments routed by larger companies from whom they buy because the larger companies make every effort to give them the lowest delivered price, and employ special skills not available in the smaller companies.

The other principal method of traffic management employed by smaller companies is to delegate these functions to an outside agency: a shippers association, a chamber of commerce, or an independent traffic consultant. These agencies maintain professional traffic staffs which perform almost all standard traffic management functions for their members or clients. There are a large number of such associations and consultant services in the

U.S. The traffic manager of the association or consultant firm is in effect the traffic manager for each of the firms served, and in some cases actually carries a title identifying him as such; there are some traffic managers who represent the shipping interests of as many as 100 or more smaller firms, a situation not unlike that of the corporate traffic manager who controls the transportation activities of as many as 300 or 400 company plants.

II—STRUCTURE OF THE TRANSPORTATION INDUSTRY

The five basic modes of transportation are *rail, highway, water, pipeline,* and *air*. The structure of the transportation industry is based on these five modes plus a number of variations and subgroups derived from (1) their several legal forms, (2) a number of auxiliary modes of transportation, and (3) various modal combinations (coordinated systems).

LEGAL FORMS

The basic legal forms of transportation carriers are *common, contract,* and *private*. The first two are often lumped together as "for-hire" carriers, indicating that they offer their services for sale to the shipping public.

Common carriers comprise the backbone of the transportation industry. They offer their services to the public at large on a shipment-by-shipment basis. All railroads, and most other carriers, fall in this category.

Contract carriers also serve the public, but in a more selective vein. They operate exclusively under contractual agreements with individual shippers, and serve only those contracting shippers on a continuing basis.

Regulation. Depending on the type of service they provide, surface modes of for-hire carriage may be either subject to, or exempt from, governmental regulation by Federal and/or state agencies. Such regulation (as administered by the Interstate Commerce Commission on the Federal level, and the various public utility and commerce commissions in the states) governs a great deal of what a carrier does: the service it provides, the commodities it carries, the routes it traverses, the rates it charges, the shippers it serves, and so forth.

Except for railroads (which, other than a few private short-line operations, are uniformly subject to regulation), the determination of whether a carrier does or does not come under regulation depends on the nature of the service it offers. Exemptions are provided by statute for, among others, motor carriers of unprocessed agricultural commodities (except bananas), motor carriers performing purely local dry service, water carriers of bulk commodities (with certain restrictions). (There are also other exemptions covering newspaper delivery trucks, school buses, hotel limousines and the like, none of which have significant bearing on commercial transportation as a whole.)

Since it is service that distinguishes regulated from unregulated transportation, it is entirely possible for the same carrier to mix both types of operations. Indeed, this is the rule for regulated contract carriers, which will frequently complement their unidirectional regulated service with "back-haul" movements of agricultural traffic in order to avoid empty runs. The carriers must comply with regulatory standards only to the extent to which they perform regulated service.

Those regulatory standards include, among other things, the filing of tariffs or schedules specifying their rate levels (which rates may not be changed without consent of the governing agency), neither expanding nor contracting service without prior approval, subjecting their finances to government and public scrutiny, and, of course, many other requirements. Both Federal and state governments also maintain safety rules with which *all* transporters, regulated and exempt alike, must comply.

It should be noted that the above descriptions of regulation pertain only to surface domestic transportation. Under legislation enacted in 1977, air cargo transportation is largely exempt from Federal regulation. Foreign oceanic commerce is under the jurisdiction of the Federal Maritime Commission.

The *private transporter* is one who hauls his own goods in his own (or leased) vehicles using his own personnel. Rather rigid restrictions on this category are maintained by the regulatory agencies, who fear the competitive effect private carriage may have on its for-hire counterpart.

MODES OF TRANSPORTATION

Auxiliary Modes. These include the U.S. Postal Service, which furnishes parcel post services; freight forwarders, who relieve shippers of responsibility of handling their own freight, but use the services of for-hire regulated carriers for the actual transportation; brokers, who perform consolidation and/or break-bulk service prior to or after the line-haul transportation takes place; and shippers' associations, which are consortiums of shippers acting in the capacity of forwarders and/or brokers for the individual shippers who comprise their membership. (For further discussion of freight forwarders and shipper's associations, see Section III of this chapter.)

The general trend in the importance of parcel post in relation to total revenues has been downward, reflecting competition from private small shipment services. Freight forwarders and brokers have continued to increase their relative importance. Freight assembled and distributed by shippers' associations has been increasing rapidly in volume in recent years.

Coordinated Systems. Coordinated systems make possible the movement of goods by two or more modes of transportation in regularly scheduled operations. Modal combinations, commonly referred to as coordinated transportation services, include *piggyback* (highway trailer on rail flatcar), *fishyback* (highway trailer on ship), *train-ship* (rail car on ship), and *air-truck* (interchange of freight between motor and air vehicles), and others.

Statistics for most coordinated transportation operations are obscured in currently-collected data. They are "divided" among participating modes because of the systems of reporting required by the Interstate Commerce Commission and Civil Aeronautics Board. However, all indications are that the use of these services is growing steadily. More and more are being instituted each year. Probably the greatest growth is in piggyback service.

Rail. Historically, rail carriers have accounted for the largest percentage of the freight tonnage moved within the United States. However, during the 1960s the railroads finally fell behind motor carriers, although they still account for an important share of the total volume. Perhaps one of the main reasons for the railroads' fall from preeminence was the growing need of shippers to move traffic in smaller lots.

The ability of the railroads to transport large quantities of freight efficiently over long distances was the primary factor which for so many years gave the railroads the largest share of transport business in the economy. The underlying importance of a sound rail system was emphasized by the tremendous part they played in the national defense effort during World War II.

Highway. Since 1930, highway carriers have developed from one-truck operations serving limited requirements into large carriers, some of which have revenues exceeding $250 million annually. In the 1950s, many motor carriers grew and became transcontinental systems. Others became large regional carriers. The flexibility of highway transportation, ranging from interstate operations to alley-to-alley movements, has given motor carriers an inherent advantage in many spheres of competition with railroads. Urban decentralization and the previously mentioned demand for relatively small-quantity shipments to many different locales (as against the far more centralized traffic pattern that existed during earlier eras) have played an important role in their development.

Water. These carriers have been faced with difficult problems of work rules, substantial increases in wage rates, and selective rate-cutting by competing modes of transportation. Even so, they have been able to maintain their share of total volume and revenues. Great Lakes traffic (excluding international shipping) has fallen in importance while inland waterways, coastwise, and intercoastal carriers have increased their share.

Pipelines. Pipelines carriers increased their percent of total transportation tonnage during the post-World War II period. The number of pipelines increased because of the demand for the movement of large volumes of liquids and gases economically.

This demand justified the expansion of existing facilities, and extensions into new areas where pipelines were not considered feasible as late as 1950.

Air. Air freight has shown the most significant increase in tonnage (percentage wise) during the same period. This increase came because the service was largely undeveloped and it had important advantages of service.

Private and Exempt. No accurate statistics are available for the volume of private and exempt transportation. It is estimated that the volume of freight handled in intercity movements by highway, the most important private mode, is roughly twice the amount reported for the highway common carriers. There are smaller amounts of private transportation by rail, water, and air.

COSTS OF OPERATION

Rail. In the railroad industry, the requirements for extensive fixed facilities (land for rights-of-way, yards, and terminals) make fixed costs a relatively high percentage of total cost. Extensive fixed facilities permit a rail carrier to operate long trains with a minimum of motive power and manpower in relation to the volume of tonnage moved, but fixed costs are higher for railroads than those of any other mode except pipeline.

Highway. Contrasted with railroads and pipelines, the truck operator has a relatively small investment in terminal facilities and operates single truck and trailer units over publicly-owned highway instead of privately-owned rights-of-way. Charges for equipment depreciation are relatively less than in other transportation industries. These two factors combine to give trucking the lowest fixed costs of any mode of transportation.

Water. Individual ships frequently exceed the cost of jet tranports, but the fixed costs of water transportation as a percentage of total cost are in most cases less than those of the airlines, although greater than those of highway carriers. If the costs of the large bulk and dry cargo terminal facilities essential to water movement were added, along with the costs of navigational aids and waterway improvement and maintenance, it is possible that the fixed costs of water movement would represent a large proportion of total cost for these carriers.

Pipeline. The fixed costs of pipeline operations include interest on land acquired or rights purchased for construction of the pipeline, depreciation of the cost of construction of the line itself, and depreciation charges against costs of constructing necessary terminals and pumping stations. Because of these large fixed cost elements, and others such as property taxes, pipelines have the greatest percentage of fixed costs of operation of any of the modes of transportation.

Air. Although the largest jet transports cost $20-plus million apiece, airline fixed costs do not represent as large a percentage of total cost as in the railroad industry. However, if airline terminal facilities were not provided by local communities (with heavy Federal Government support), and airways were not established and sustained by the Federal Aviation Administration, the percentage of fixed costs of air carriers would probably exceed those of railroads.

Coordinated Systems. Ordinarily the costs of operation in a coordinated transportation system are less than the costs of one of the participating modes and more than the costs of the other participating mode. But sometimes total costs are lowered because of the coordinated operation. This was true in the case of piggyback in some instances. Piggyback and other types of coordination have tended to flourish because of improved service thus made available and the tendency to use each mode for the type of service in which it is inherently more efficient.

CONTAINERIZATION

Containerization refers to the practice of packing goods so as to eliminate unnecessary rehandling. Containers are commonly fitted with fixtures which allow them to be transferred easily from one mode of transportation to another. Containerization of some type is necessary to development of the full potential of most coordinated transportation services.

Containers have generally provided their users with: (1) lower handling costs (resulting in lower freight rates), (2) lower in-transit insurance costs, (3) reduced in-transit damage, and (4) reduced pilferage. These advantages have been offset somewhat by the cost of containers, the general lack of adequate facilities for handling them, and the problems of empty containers resulting from traffic imbalance. The pace of containerization has sometimes been slowed by obsolescent work rules and labor reluctance to change those rules.

Usage. Containers are currently used by all major modes of transportation except pipeline. They range in size from the 160-cubic-foot type used typically by firms moving goods in international trade to containers of about 2,500 cubic feet that are used in domestic highway-rail, rail-water, and highway-water coordinated service.

Containers are replacing other types of equipment, particularly the highway trailer, in coordinated transportation. It is likely that much of the trailer-on-flat-car movements made today will be converted to container-on-flat-car movements in the future. The development of detachable axles and other features have made this possible. Further economic reasons for this substitution include: (1) elimination of multi-state highway licensing, (2) special routing requirements called for by limited clearances for piggyback trailers, (3) off-balance load characteristics and high center of gravity of trailers on flat cars, (4) lower train speeds required by unbalanced trailer loads, and (5) equipment purchase savings. Some of these same economic savings dictate the current and future use of containers in other forms of coordinated transportation as well.

III—TRANSPORTATION SERVICES

FREIGHT FORWARDERS

A freight forwarder performs all facets of transportation except the actual, physical line-haul movement. For the latter it employs the services of "underlying" air, motor, rail, and water carriers.

Most forwarder business in the United States is handled by *sur-*

face freight forwarders—those that make use of rail and motor exclusively for line-haul transportation. They handle relatively low-weight shipments which would fall into the category of less-than-truckload (LTL) or less-than-carload (LCL) traffic. They assess rates closely comparable to the motor carriers' LTL and the railroads' LCL rate levels. Their profit, after they consolidate the freight they receive and turn it over to line-haul rail or motor carriers for physical transportation, comes from the difference between LTL/LCL rates they charge their customers and the truckload/carload rates they pay the underlying line-haul carriers. Thus, the entire forwarder industry is built on the transportation industry's economies of scale, which dictate reduced rate levels for larger quantities of freight.

In all respects except the actual physical haulage of goods, the freight forwarding company acts in the capacity of carrier. It assumes full origin-to-destination responsibility for the shipments tendered it, issues a through bill of lading, provides (either itself or through local drayage companies) pickup-and-delivery service, handles any required tracing of shipments while in transit, and otherwise maintains full control of the entire origin-to-destination movement. In the event of in-transit loss or damage, the shipper legally looks only to the forwarder for settlement of claims; it is up to the forwarder to obtain such settlements as it can, for its own account, from the line-haul carrier(s).

Surface freight forwarders must obtain operating authority from the Interstate Commerce Commission for any interstate service they provide. Air freight forwarders, which provide similar services by use of underlying airlines and are known as "indirect air carriers," require no regulatory authority under a 1977 law deregulating air cargo traffic, and operate on a strict market-competition basis.

Freight forwarders generally offer direct through transportation service between major industrial and commercial centers, consolidating shipments at the point of origin and distributing them at the destination. Their personnel are highly skilled in transportation procedures, and can often secure for the shipper faster and better transportation service than he can obtain through his own independent efforts. They also relieve the shipper of the burden of considerable documentation.

Many forwarders specialize in certain types of traffic, or particular types of service. For example, some forwarders deal almost exclusively in "piggyback" (trailer-onrail-flatcar) transportation; their capabilities in these areas of specialization are usually broader than those of the individual shipper. A number of forwarders also operate private communications systems to facilitate the tracing and expediting of shipments.

Foreign Freight Forwarders. Foreign freight forwarders operate in essentially the same fashion as domestic forwarders, except that they generally offer export-import services in connection with documentation, consular invoices, etc. Ocean freight forwarders differ in that they actually receive fees from the shippers they serve, and are permitted to serve as brokers for shipping lines, receiving a commission from the latter in addition to the shipper's fee. For the small shipper exporting or importing via ocean carrier, the services of a foreign freight forwarder in documentation, credit, export packing, and Customs requirements are particularly valuable.

To the extent that they perform operations within the United States, ocean forwarders are regulated by the Federal Maritime Commisssion (and are classed as "NVOs"—"non-vessel operators").

SHIPPERS' ASSOCIATIONS

Cooperative shipping by industrial firms under certain circumstances can be a significant method of reducing transportation costs. Since transportation involves the public interest, Congress considered it wise in 1942 to add Section 402 (c) (1) to the Interstate Commerce Act, to permit manufacturers or other commercial enterprises which ship goods interstate to band together and arrange volume shipments. Group shipping was practiced before 1942 however, and began to expand in 1937 when the railroads published an all-commondity rate (carload mixture of different articles) to encourage volume shipping. This liberalization of rail tariffs helped large retail department store companies particularly because of their steady flow of traffic to their scattered outlets. The rapid growth of associations in the late 1950s and the 1960s was aided by the introduction of rail "piggyback" services and "freight all kinds" rates.

At the outset of this shipping innovation some companies held back using them for fear of revealing customer names and sales volume to competitors in the pool. But when distant markets were cut off by freight costs and minimum shipments became prohibitive, potential users joined in pursuit of a common goal—sales at low delivery prices.

This arrangement is advantageous for companies shipping less-than-carload lots between metropolitan areas more than approximately 600 miles apart, where carload rates offer sizeable economies—sometimes half the less carload rates.

The shippers' association operates like a freight forwarder in assembling small shipments, consolidating them into carload or truckload lots, and distributing the individual shipments to the proper destinations. But the similarity ends there because the freight forwarder (1) is an independent firm, (2) is in business for profit, (3) is a common carrier subject to Federal regulation, (4) collects less-than-carload rates and minimum charges from the shipper and pays the railroad carload rates for its transportation service on the long haul, and (5) generally covers a wider area.

When freight rates began to increase rapidly after World War II, new associations spread quickly and now number well over 100. The American Institute for Shippers' Associations, Inc., was organized to coordinate the activities of its members as well as to preserve and protect their rights.

Some shippers' associations have failed, mainly because of insufficient tonnage and poor planning. Regularity of car forwarding is important, because sacrifice of service to members may jeopardize sales, thereby defeating the original marketing purpose.

Some associations become involved in investigations of—and even prosecutions for—ICC violations or improper practices. Shippers or associations and carriers are equally liable to many of the penalty provisions of the Act.

Generally the nature or classification of merchandise for shipment is not restricted, provided the commodity is packed well and can be loaded without danger of damage to other lading. Associations are usually formed by companies shipping similar merchandise. Membership is not limited in number, since tonnage must be sufficient to ship full cars to a central point as a practical matter.

The ICC has recommended various amendments to Congress to tighten exempt provision relating to shippers' associations to eliminate from operation other than bona fide, non-profit shipper groups. Legislators have turned a deaf ear to such suggestions primarily because of heavy shipper opposition.

Advantages gained through successful group shipping are: reduced total freight costs; fast and reliable delivery service; no penalty for small shipments; minimum stocks because of constant flow of merchandise from manufacturers to stores; shipments pinpointed through manifest tracing; and in most cases, reduced claims through systematic freight handling.

Local chambers of commerce or trade groups in most large cities will usually assist in organizing shippers' associations. However, no company without a full-time traffic manager or the help of a transportation consultant should attempt to form one.

10
Packaging

The proper location of the package development function within a company will depend upon the type of business activity. Businesses predominantly in drugs, foods, and cosmetics are oriented more toward marketing and research than toward engineering, and find it logical to locate the package development function in Marketing or as a special staff operation. Package development for industrial products, hardware, appliances, and products which require protective shipping or have special use features, is often in Engineering or Production.

ORGANIZATION

The handling of a package development program can range from a part-time job of a buyer, a limited function of an engineer, researcher, or graphic-arts expert, to the full-time responsibility of a Director of Package Development.

Where the total reponsibility is not delegated to one individual, the function is split among various departments. Often this means a Package Committee, composed of the heads of each department involved. The committee approach is being utilized less frequently. The trend now is to professionalization—requiring a Packaging Director or Coordinator of Packaging.

The qualifications necessary for the person responsible for the function will vary with each industry. However, he must know packaging materials, components, methods, and equipment. In establishing personnel requirements, consideration should be given to the routine functions which may be conducted presently by other departments but which could be transferred to package development. For a rule of thumb, a company with 200 employees should have at least one person specializing in package development. With the use of a scheduling system, one trained individual can directly supervise many technicians in a packaging department.

SCOPE

A complete packaging program includes: (1) planning and coordination of package development activities throughout the organization; (2) conducting research; (3) developing and engineering; (4) testing; (5) writing specifications; (6) selecting and controlling color; (7) controlling the quality of packaging components; (8) assembling and storing of information, samples, etc.; and (9) analyzing packaging (return goods and value analysis).

An effective initial procedure is to list current packaging activities, problems, and projects throughout the company. This list will help answer such questions as: How much duplication of effort occurs? Do any records of value exist? Are they organized for easy reference?

Planning and Coordinating Package Development. There is no established program for all industry with respect to the planning and coordination of package development. However, a review of the following functions will indicate the advantages of establishing a focal point for proper control.

Product Data. For a new product, product data must be obtained from Research (or, if necessary, produced by the package development group). A product-data check list should be designed, covering all pertinent aspects of the product, including special processing (if container and product are processed simultaneously), special protection required during shelf life, special packing protection, dispensing, and the like.

Package Data. Information to be sought here includes:
(1) Detailed description of the uses of the product, the condi-

tions under which it is used, the type of user, and any supplementary devices used with the product.

(2) Sizes, possible combinations of packages, sample packages, special packages for particular markets, and the various put-ups required.

(3) Predicted volume: minimum order quantities for packaging components below which costs begin to soar, so that materials with prohibitive costs can be eliminated early.

(4) Processing of product and existing packaging facilities; special processing (sterilization, vacuum packaging, etc.); automated equipment and machine limitations.

(5) Channels of distribution: requirements for storage, shipping, handling, marketing, etc.

(6) Promotional requirements: The package should almost always be designed with features which will draw attention and please the consumer. Promotional requirements are dictated by the channel of distribution, advertising media, and type of consumer. Increasingly, consumer-convenience features are being incorporated in the package to provide an added factor for promotion, to extend penetration into new markets, and to encourage more effective product use.

(7) Legal requirements: legal aspects of the copy; patentable devices; Food and Drug Administration approval, deceptive packaging; etc.

(8) Research or pharmacological requirements, where applicable: sterility, design of anatomical devices, dosages, and similar aspects.

(9) Labeling, use directions, recipes. (Often these are the most important means of producing repeat use as well as initial sales.)

Package Research. From information and samples it is possible to screen a new material or package for application in the product lines. Testing of all or even many new materials is, of course, not practical. By comparing the advantages of both the present material and a new candidate, many reasons why the material should or should not be tested will become obvious. Reasons for eliminating a new material from consideration include:

(1) It lacks one or more absolute requirements of the package,

such as clarity, ease of tear, flexibility, etc. However, one should determine whether modifications might not overcome the problem.

(2) While it has the required characteristics, it is more expensive than the present material.

(3) It offers all advantages of the present material and is less costly, but the yearly volume is so small that the cost of testing would not be justified.

(4) If accepted, it would require the purchase of new packaging equipment that could not be justified by anticipated volume.

Development and Engineering. Systematic procedures will simplify the determination of the right package from the great mass of materials, components, ideas, methods, and cost variations available. After it has been shown that necessary requirements will be satisfied, additional features can be incorporated.

Materials. From the product data covered previously, suitable materials must be determined. A review of files, catalogs, and published charts may produce a list of potential materials. However, it is sometimes necessary to search the supplier market (laminators, liner manufacturers, basic plastic-resin manufacturers) for materials with particular characteristics. All potential materials must be further classified by advantages and disadvantages. For example, a transparent film may afford superior appearance (and eventual sales) but have a higher cost than a foil laminate. Materials with the greatest advantages must be tested under controlled simulated storage, shipping, use, and other important conditions. A similar process is used to determine the material for devices, intermediate packaging, and shipping containers.

Design. With the material selected, the type of packaging which may be manufactured is limited to available manufacturing processes (molding, extruding, laminating, etc.). Again, exploration, testing, and screening are necessary to determine which type of package—tube, can, dish, lamination, etc.—is best. Dimensional and design characteristics must be determined in relation to the requirements listed previously. Convenience features for dispensing or use should be investigated. Most package development departments have a collection of idea-stimulating sources. Visits to retail establishments (for consumer packaging ideas) are fruitful.

Available services of suppliers should be utilized, where possible, for preliminary tests and screening. It is sometimes necessary to obtain the services of commercial laboratories and consultants.

Copy. Sales promotion and research usually determine original copy for printed items. Package development must constantly check for size, color, copy, location of printing, and quality of workmanship.

Time. With experience, it is possible to estimate the time required to complete a development. Periodic recording of time needed to perform isolated development functions will furnish a valuable reference.

Testing. Package development performs two types of tests. First, performance claims made by suppliers must be verified. Second, functional tests determine whether a proposed package can withstand the rigors of processing, distribution, use, and environmental conditions of storage and retailing. Ideally, the entire life of the package should be simulated. However, experienced package development personnel can predict the durability and suitability of many materials and components under various conditions.

It is wise to permit the same individual to conduct all similar tests within one project. In this way, subjective values reported will be consistent and comparable.

Specifications. After development and approval, complete specifications must be prepared. At the minimum, the specifications should protect against use of packaging which does not meet the requirements in function, quality, or assurance of constant quality. Exacting, high-speed equipment, secondary processing (autoclaving, etc.), color matching of components, severe handling or storage conditions, and the like are common in today's large-scale packaging operations. Failure in any one of these can affect the others.

Each specification should be labeled as *critical, major,* or *minor*. The acceptable quality level (AQL) can be established on this classification. Where many variations of one type of component are involved, it may be simpler to develop a manual which lists all similar specifications, with a supplemental sheet indicating the individual differences.

Color Standards. Color standards can be established by (1) accumulating present stock samples, (2) requesting a special run from a supplier, (3) requesting standards through the supplier's ink house, or (4) having them printed by a local printer. Northern daylight is the established light under which color matching is performed. Once color standards have been established, spectrophotometric readings can be obtained from the ink house for a small fee. This will enable a matching of the original colors, which are apt to change over extended periods of time. (The Container Corporation of America has developed a "Color Harmony Manual" to aid in color selection and control.)

Quality Control. Spot checks do not produce scientific quality information. It is advisable to establish a statistical inspection program. Where funds or labor are limited, this could be restricted initially to critical aspects. Newly established quality control programs should allow for easy adjustments in specifications. Tolerances should be firmly established only after rechecking their validity.

Information and Samples. Information files are set up under several broad categories: (1) basic materials; (2) type of component; (3) activities (e.g., testing, specification-writing, scheduling methods, etc.); (4) suppliers; (5) machinery and equipment; (6) specific subjects (color tables and charts, etc.). Samples may save thousands of words. Samples can be filed or stored in two categories: (1) materials; and (2) type of component.

Project files, test-report files, and specification files complete the major information aspects.

Packaging Analysis. The magnitude and complexity of package development call for constant vigilance. One barometer of packaging is the condition of returned goods. A periodic review of these will indicate necessary changes. A check with other companies will indicate a norm which should be expected in such things as bottle breakage, leakage of liquids, container failures, etc. High returns are, of course, danger signals. The general appearance and function of packaging should also be evaluated periodically. And occasional visits to retailers, wholesalers, distributors, and other segments of a distribution cycle will often uncover areas for improvement or cost reduction.

(Note: *Modern Packaging Encyclopedia,* published annually by *Modern Packaging,* New York, contains sections on package planning and development, materials, containers, printing and labeling, shipping and protection, machinery, and buyers' directory.)

Value Analysis. A periodic review of each component of packaging in use will indicate many areas where substitution and change are possible. These include (1) material composition; (2) size; (3) design; and (4) finish. Cost savings are often possible through standardization, and occasionally, by eliminating obsolete requirements. (See Chapter 5, VALUE ENGINEERING.)

PACKAGING PROTECTION

With rare exceptions, commodities entering the physical distribution chain require at least some protection against the stresses they may expect to suffer en route to their point of consumption.

This is the archetypal function of *protection packaging:* to guard the goods against intransit damage. Most frequently the damage feared is of a purely physical nature: breakage, dents, etc., due to buffeting and rough handling. There are, however, other types of damage which must be guarded against in specific circumstances. For example, foodstuffs and certain other products must be protected against spoilage, contamination, and the like.

Especially within the past decade, a new element has entered the field of protective packaging. It has become widely recognized that packaging techniques may be employed to achieve significant economies in the physical distribution process. This function is exemplified by that most efficient of packages, the large intermodal container, which can travel as an unchanged unit from one carrier to another—truck to train to ship or plane.

Protection against Crime. A relatively new role for protective packaging relates to the increased incidence of crime in the public transportation system. Packaging techniques may be employed either to render theft-susceptible goods more difficult to steal (generally through unitization into large aggregates too cumbersome for the casual thief), or to disguise their nature. Manufacturers and vendors of television sets, radios, wristwatches, jewelry, electronic components, alcoholic liquors, tobacco products, automotive parts and accessories, etc.—traditionally among the most tempting goods to thieves—are increasingly marking their packages in codes, with all advertising removed, in an effort to thwart the criminals.

The degree and type of packaging needed depends almost totally on the nature of the goods being moved. Where the damage sought to be protected against is physical, industrial packaging engineers seek to determine impact points, areas of weakness, and other shipping characteristics in order to design the optimum packaging system. Among the materials available for use in containers are cardboard, corrugated paperboard, wood, wood-and-wire combinations, metal, plastic, styrofoam, etc. Numerous other commodities ranging from the traditional crumpled newspapers and excelsior to sophisticated (and reusable) cellulose and plastic foam substances, may be employed as dunnage, in order further to cushion the product against harm. Shrink-wrap and vacuum-pack systems are used to protect perishables where necessary.

Containerized Shipping. From the standpoint of protection, the intermodal container is a highly utilitarian form of packaging. Its structural strength affords the most complete protection against physical damage; it may be refrigerated or subjected to atmospheric control to prevent contamination or spoilage of perishables, and its size and strength will deter all but the most ambitious and determined of thieves.

In addition to this, the container affords the potential for major physical distribution economies. Its size and weight brings transportation economies-of-scale within reach, and the normal low loss-and-damage claims ratios provide a further economic incentive. For-hire transportation firms have generally recognized these advantages by establishing especially low rate levels on goods moving in containers, to the economic benefit of their customers as well as themselves.

Unfortunately, certain problems continue to beset containerization. Internecine conflicts within the transportation community, and outmoded legal restrictions imposed on that community, limit the use of containers in many cases. Theoretically, a containerized shipment is capable of portal-to-portal movement via any combination of rail, motor, or water carriage; and "jumbo jet" aircraft are technologically capable of joining in this *de facto* consortium of modes. However, carrier or regulatory restrictions on container interchange, union insistence on needlessly unloading and repacking the containers in some cases, and similar occurrences deprive containerization of a good deal of its potential. Hopefully, these limitations will diminish in the course of time, permitting at least a closer approach to the full potential.

Unitization. Containerization is actually just one aspect of a broader approach to the problem of packaging which goes under the generic name "unitization." Pallets, airline "igloos," modular containers of various sorts, cargo nets, and other instrumentalities are also used to achieve similar objectives. Behind these developments runs the basic attitude that the larger and more enclosed a package becomes, the more easily, safely, and economically it may be shipped.

The same trend is visible in the handling of bulk commodities. Specially designed bulk carriers, of all modes, are growing increasingly larger and more sophisticated; at once they offer greater protection to the commodities being shipped, and a greater potential for consolidation into ever larger units of shipment. Among the more interesting developments in this area is the tendency to employ bulk-handling methods wherever possible, sometimes in instances where they would not appear on the surface to be applicable. Even that reputedly "perfect" natural package, the eggshell, has been discarded in the interests of bulk unitization; raw eggs are now shelled at or near their origin, and shipped on to destination in refrigerated liquid bulk vehicles.

Because of this broader role, packaging is becoming increasingly interwoven into the physical distribution management system. Packaging determinations are most often made within a company's physical distribution or traffic department, in recognition of the major role packaging can play with regard to physical distribution and transportation costs. In this systems approach, protective packaging is regarded as a physical distribution subsystem, which both affects and is affected by other subsystems such as traffic/transportation, material handling, warehousing, inventory control, and so forth.

As an example of how these factors are inseparably affiliated with protective packaging, it is clearly impossible to design or procure an efficient material handling system without reference to the form in which the company's goods are packaged. It is equally impossible to establish a warehouse operation without regard to packaging, or to effectuate inventory control procedures. To be sure, sales/marketing and production considerations enter into decisions concerning protective packaging, but for the majority of industrial concerns its most important affiliation is to the physical distribution area of operations.

11
Warehousing

Warehousing—the storage and protection of raw materials and/or finished goods—has come to be regarded as a key element in marketing strategy.

Most industrial firms include both company-owned (private) and public warehouses in their distribution systems. A few companies use all private or all public warehouses, and there are some that use a single public warehouse as a "control" on the cost/service performance of their own system of privately operated warehouses.

SCOPE

The prime purpose of warehousing activity is of course strategic deployment of marketable goods in such a way as to minimize total distribution costs and maximize customer service. Determining the optimum number, location and size of warehouses for any given company is a highly complex matter, however, involving a great deal more than cheap land and a proximity to markets. In fact, some companies have found it practical to do away with regionalized warehousing altogether and have switched to premium transportation, air or truck, to render a level of customer service comparable to that offered by an extensive network of warehouses.

One reason in particular why many managements make careful studies of their companies' warehousing patterns goes even beyond the cost of the warehousing operation itself; this is the cost of carrying inventory, both the actual physical handling costs and the costs of invested capital. These inventory costs have been found to run as high as 25% of the value of the finished goods; where goods have a high per-pound value or where there is infrequent customer demand, these costs can eat deeply into potential profits.

Traditionally, warehouses have been located to serve areas conforming with sales territories, often as the direct responsibility of the regional sales managers. This picture has largely changed, as the increasing use of sophisticated mathematic analysis (see case example in the Appendix) shows that territories which are good from a sales management point of view are often inefficient and costly from a distribution point of view. Moreover, there is a definite trend to relieve sales management personnel of warehousing responsibilities which may conflict with their primary duties.

Where the distribution center concept has been adopted, warehousing operations tend to be under the central control of a warehousing/transportation/inventory control executive who may be the head of a distinct warehousing department (particularly true in companies with several hundred or more warehouses) or at the head of warehousing activities within a distribution department. In many companies, the warehousing function—both private and public—is placed in the traffic department because of the close relationship between the transportation and warehousing functions, with numerous transportation privileges like storage in transit, processing in transit, free switching, etc., having a direct bearing on warehousing operation.

TRADE—OFFS

The fact that use of warehouses enables companies to take advantage of volume transportation rates for long-haul shipments has long been at the heart of the entire warehousing operation, but current thinking places it on the same level with inventory costs and competitive advantage. In exploration of total costs, for example, companies have found that it is more practical to increase the speed of order processing (through teletype, telephone, and data processing systems) and eliminate various of their warehouses, while continuing to render the same level of customer service. A major company, Westinghouse, took this approach some years ago, and reduced inventory in one item alone from $5 million to $2 million, at the same time closing a number of its field warehouses. If order time could be reduced by twenty-four hours, the company reasoned, customers could be served from warehouses twenty-four hours more distant and the problem of maintaining complete stocks at numerous locations could be more easily solved.

While it is true that sales and marketing management still tend to feel that opening new warehouses is a good competitive tool, and usually resist warehouse closings and relocations, it is rapidly being demonstrated by many companies that competitive advantage and customer service improve with scientific management of warehouses as part of a complete system.

There are numerous points of view as to the relative merits of private warehouses vs. public. While the direct charges for public warehousing space are generally found to be higher than those involved in private warehousing, public warehousing offers a good deal more flexibility with no fixed charges, as discussed later herein. At the same time, private warehousing offers the advantage of special tailoring of equipment and facilities to a company's products, something that is not always possible with public warehouses. On the other hand, a number of public warehousing companies are adopting the "distribution center" concept for their own operations and, in addition to using highly sophisticated order-picking and handling equipment, also have data processing systems for order processing, inventory control, and even customer billing on behalf of their clients. In some cases these warehouses perform such finishing operations as unit packaging of bulk materials, labeling, pricing, etc., and furnish display and office space for their clients.

As a management function, responsibility for warehousing operations is rapidly becoming of major importance in total marketing and distribution. Although it is doubtful that many companies will create executive posts for this single operation, it is likely that whoever is resposible for the function will carry considerable weight in all major distribution decisions.

THE PUBLIC WAREHOUSE

As trade and commerce broadened, there developed the opportunity and need for facilities in which someone will take care of property *for others,* temporarily. Thus we have the business of public warehousing. It is an old business. Public warehousing transactions took place in the Middle Ages at Venice and Genoa. Wherever there is trade and commerce, there is need for public warehousing, and the service is now provided in every country.

Warehouses in Modern Distribution. In the United States, with its free flow of trade and intense competition, manufacturers and distributors bid for sales in markets throughout the nation. To meet competition, both price-wise and service-wise, alert and efficient distribution is a prime necessity. As to service, no method of shipping can improve on having goods already in the market—the maintenance of "spot stocks" at diversified and strategic locations.

The manufacturer is, therefore, faced with the need of determining whether he will build, buy, or lease a branch warehouse for operation by his own personnel, or whether he will use a public warehouse. For many companies the latter has been found to have numerous pronounced advantages. Perhaps the most important of these is flexibility. But before discussing this factor, six other specific advantages are briefly listed here:

(1) Space-Cost Economy. Year-round maintenance costs, heat, light, taxes, etc., that apply to company-owned facilities regardless of degree of utilization are of no concern to the user of public warehouses. Storage charges are made on a per package, per hundredweight, or other unit basis per month.

(2) Labor Economy. Trends toward guaranteed pay plans create a serious situation where wide seasonal variations are inherent in either production or sales. The manufacturer must maintain level

production, and, as later explained, the public warehouseman helps him accomplish this. Handling charges are "per unit" in a public warehouse, thereby assessing labor costs only as they are actually incurred.

(3) Transportation Efficiency. Shipping in carload or truckload quantity to public warehouses and distributing to local and nearby areas from warehouse stocks saves the shipper the difference between LCL and carload rates, an appreciable transportation cost factor.

(4) Reduced Investment. Even where only the bare essentials are provided, capital investment in a company-owned warehouse building is substantial. The user of a public warehouse avoids tying up large sums in fixed assets.

(5) Accurate Cost Prediction. The warehouseman's tariff or quotation permits accurate prediction and budgeting of distribution cost for each unit of merchandise.

(6) Sales Efficiency. Often a salesman located at a branch house finds himself tied down with the administrative detail of running the establishment. The public warehouse provides office space and services for the salesman but frees him from all non-selling detail.

Flexibility. Some companies have small amounts of merchandise to store and distribute; others find that in a given area their need may run to the storage and handling of hundreds of carloads. Usually these needs vary widely throughout the year. Use of public warehouse facilities can exactly match the needs of the moment.

Shifting population and decentralization of merchandising centers and industrial facilities create a need for a mobile distribution system. The volume handled through a given distribution point may drop in favor of another. The public warehousing industry, represented in every marketing center of the United States, provides the immediate mobility necessary.

Another need for flexibility is found in changing transportation requirements. Whatever mode of transportation is necessary for a particular shipment, the warehousing industry is located and equipped to adapt itself to its customers' needs.

Finally, efficient warehousing demands a versatility of types of space. Some storage needs are best served in multi-story buildings, others in single-story facilities. Some commodities need controlled conditions of temperature or humidity. The public warehouseman is able to furnish or arrange for the facility most suited to the storage, handling, and distribution of each product.

The Production Function and Warehousing. The public warehouse is of importance to others than those directly concerned with distribution. Advantageous purchases of raw materials and components can be made, and the items can be held, pending use, in a public merchandise warehouse local to the factory; subassemblies and component parts can be delivered to the assembly line by the local warehouseman as needed; and elimination of other than immediate daily storage needs at both ends of the production line can free up additional area for new production facilities.
Blending of Peaks and Valleys. The historical association of production and consumption with periods of peaks and valleys does not fit in with the modern business concept of optimum use of productive facilities. In steps taken to alleviate this situation, the necessity of providing customer service at minimum cost cannot be overlooked. It is here that public warehousing blends the fluctuating requirements of many manufacturers into a reasonably constant volume, allowing maximum utilization of facilities.

Distribution. Two basic conditions inherent in public warehousing make for efficiency in distribution:

(1) The ability to pool the distribution needs of many companies makes it possible to eliminate pronounced peaks and valleys.

(2) The large-scale storage and handling operation permits the economic utilization of specialized facilities and personnel.

A graphic, though simplified, exposition of the dovetailing process used is shown in Exhibit I. Each company's varied requirements for storage space are combined in the public warehouse. Company A, for example, would need 25,000 square feet of storage space for March and October peaks, and during

June would use less than 5,000 square feet. Operation of its own storage and distribution facilities would require building, equipment, and personnel geared to the maximum requirement. Comparable variations exist in the distribution needs of the other companies. In June, Company B needs 37,500 square feet; in December, Company C uses 40,500 square feet; and in March Company D requires 50,000 square feet. The public warehouseman meets all of these needs with a physical plant of 100,000 square feet, yet individually operated storage and distribution facilities would require a total of 153,000 square feet to meet separate company peak requirements.

Public warehousing services are available to small and large users. From a pick-up truckload to a trainload, the warehouseman handles the requirements of each of his customers, and it is the combination of small and large needs that enables him to operate at a high degree of efficiency. Similarly, comparable savings accrue in labor and equipment costs.

Lest there be any misunderstanding of the term "blending," it is emphasized that the public warehouseman keeps the goods of each customer separate, provides the individual care required by each commodity, and maintains exact stock records on every item in his custody. His responsibility under the law is to exercise, with regard to goods in his custody, the same care "as a reasonably careful owner of similar goods would exercise."

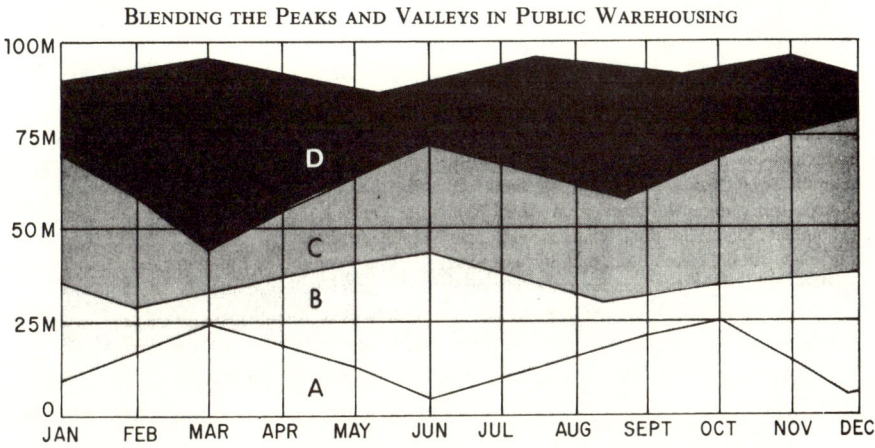

EXHIBIT I
BLENDING THE PEAKS AND VALLEYS IN PUBLIC WAREHOUSING

Additional Services. In conjunction with the services of storage and handling, the public warehouseman performs numerous "branch house" and "branch office" functions for his customers. These include such services as supplying office and display space; special clerical and telephone service; traffic information rates on all transportation, and distribution of pool cars and consolidated shipments; break-bulk operations, including packaging and assembly; physical inventories; C.O.D. collections; maintenance of and delivery to accredited customer lists; prepaying of freight bills; and loans on stored commodities.

Warehouse Receipts as Collateral. When inventories are made up of marketable commodities and cash is needed to finance increased purchases or production, *warehouse receipts* issued by responsible warehousemen provide acceptable collateral for loans to reliable principals. Under the Uniform Commercial Code, this type of financing is a well established business procedure.

BONDED WAREHOUSES

In the terminology relating to the warehousing industry, the words "bonded warehouse" probably are least understood by the general public, and by many businessmen. Despite continuing educational efforts by bankers and warehousemen, the erroneous belief persists that only warehouse receipts issued by a "bonded" warehouse are acceptable as collateral, or that a bonded warehouse, *per se,* affords some special security not afforded by an unbonded warehouse.

There are two types of United States bonded warehouses: *Customs Bonded* and *Internal Revenue Bonded* houses, neither of which affords any bonded protection to the depositor of the goods. The bond in each of these instances is to the Federal Government to protect it against nonpayment of duties or taxes.

In twenty-two states, warehousemen may be "bonded" or licensed under state regulation. In some, the bonding or licensing requirement is little more than a revenue producing measure, while in others the existence of the bonding statute and the posting of a bond by the warehouseman may mean that some degree of inspection is undertaken by state authorities.

A third classification of bonded warehouses are those for agricultural products, licensed under the United States Warehouse Act. This is a category that is of little concern to the business community and is therefore not discussed here.

12
Industrial Distributors

Industrial distributors are sometimes referred to as "The Supermarket for Industry." They are, for a large variety of industrial goods, the single most important channel of distribution from manufacturer to industrial user, performing functions of true utilitarian value. In the absence of distributors, these functions must be passed on to either the manufacturer or the industrial user. Thus industrial distributors serve to keep the lines of supply and distribution between industrial producers and industrial users from becoming hopelessly tangled.

FORMAL DEFINITION

Industrial distribution concerns the marketing of industrial supplies and equipment. These goods are used by factories, mines, railroads, mills, utilities, and other facilities in the operation of their businesses. Industrial supplies and equipment do not include raw materials or assemblies (except for standard parts, such as fasteners), but do include small equipment, tools, parts, and other supply items used in daily production, operation, and maintenance. Today these items are more commonly referred to as maintenance, repair, and operating (MRO) supplies. Industrial distributors also stock and sell standardized shop equipment such as lathes, drill presses, pipe threading equipment, pumps and compressors, and the like.

Today's industrial distributor is a local independent businessman who sells and services supplies to industries in his market area. The reason for his existence is that he can perform a far more effective job than the manufacturer can in merchandising a particular line of industrial products at the local level. In fact, the service provided by the industrial distributor actually adds value to the product as sold. This "value added" concept is a key principle in industrial distribution.

A partial list of the varied products sold by industrial distributors includes: abrasives; cutting tools; saws and files; hand pumps, valves, and compressors; power transmission equipment; industrial rubber goods; material handling equipment; air and hydraulic equipment; precision measuring tools; tubing; tool steel; and bearing stock.

The industrial distributor keeps in constant contact with his customers' top management, purchasing managers, engineers, maintenance foremen, and stockroom and shop personnel. His awareness of their problems and needs makes him a logical distribution channel from manufacturer to user. He is known by a variety of names locally which perhaps best define who the industrial distributor really is: mill supply house; industrial distributor; factory, foundry, mill, mine, oil well, contractor, marine, railway or textile supply house; hardware wholesaler; automotive jobber; construction equipment distributor; plumbing and heating wholesaler; electrical wholesaler; aircraft supply distributor; machinery and equipment dealer.

HISTORY

The field of industrial distribution generally dates back a little more than 100 years. Before that time most industrial distributor firms were not much more than hardware peddlers operating out of covered wagons. But as many of these peddlers found they could serve the new industries then starting up, they settled down nearby and began concentrating their sales efforts in those directions. For a long period there were, however, few distributors, and those that did exist often sent their salesmen on extended trips of several months, calling on plants across the country.

Industrial distributors really came into their own with the advent of standardized parts and machinery. It must be remembered that in heavy engineered installations where total unit sales are large, it is often advantageous for the manufacturer to perform all the functions himself. But as regards standardized items, e.g. light machine tools and other forms of accessory equipment, perishable productions tools and many other maintenance items and industrial supplies, industrial buyers are in the habit of purchasing on a day-to-day basis. So the mill supply house was born, the one that carried everything.

A more recent development has been the emergence of the specialized distributor. This is a firm that concentrates on only one line or service, such as bearings, valves and fittings, fasteners, or mechanical power transmission equipment.

The limited lines or departmentalized distributor also exists. He is essentially a compromise between a specialized house and a general line, or mill supply, distributor.

OPERATIONS

Many general line houses are slimming down their lines and becoming more departmentalized. Limited line houses are either becoming specialists or general line houses. Specialized distributors are adding more lines. No discernable pattern is yet clear.

The industry has in recent years continued to experience a profit squeeze, with average net profit after taxes as low as one-third of one percent. A number of factors have been responsible for this profit squeeze. Vicious price cutting is one. Increasing operating costs another. Dual distribution, that is competition for sales from their manufacturer-suppliers, another. Consequently, many industrial distributors have gone in for profitability analysis of their lines and customers, weeding out and discarding those lines and customers which do not add to their profit picture.

A manufacturer selling through industrial distributors must realize that he not only is competing against other manufacturers who make the same product, but he is also competing for the distributor's time and attention against all the manufacturers whom the distributor represents. Therefore some understanding of what distributors want is in order. This is best stated in the "Statement of Policy" formulated by the National Industrial Distributors Association and the Southern Industrial Distributors Association:

> Manufacturers should firmly establish and clearly *state in writing* (italics supplied) their expected relationship with distributors. Distributors feel that selective distribution, limited by actual market potential, should be applied to those items requiring specialized sales training and/or heavy inventory investment. Distributors feel that manufacturer, distributor and consumer will all benefit by this through greater sales activity and interest, a better chance for a fair return on inventory investment, and more competent application of such products to the consumer's need.
>
> Appointment of distributors on a selective basis should be made only after a thorough study of the distributor's sales ability and financial responsibility. Contracts between manufacturer and distributor should contain a clause providing that upon termination by either party, all goods of current design in distributor's stock are returnable at distributor's cost, with return transportation cost to be paid by the cancelling party.
>
> Those manufacturers who, totally or largely, use industrial distributors as their sales and warehousing divisions should not weaken this important arm of their business by pricing their distributors out of the O.E.M. market or by reserving large volume industries or accounts to themselves.

The industrial distributor's single most important customer is the firm engaged in metalworking. Other important customer groups are woodworking industries, public utilities, governmental agencies, agriculture equipment industries, retail hardware stores, contractors, textile industries, mines and quarries, paper manufacturers, and petroleum refiners.

TRENDS

Several noticeable trends in industrial selling have been emerging. Most significant is systems contracts, also known as systems selling or blanket contracts or orders. Under this arrangement, a customer signs a blanket order for his requirements with his local industrial distributor. The distributor agrees that he will always have on hand the tools or materials needed by his customer. He relieves the latter of the need to be concerned with complex purchase order forms, warehousing, inventory-taking, and other costs of purchasing and possession. In return, the distributor is guaranteed a market for his products.

Leasing is another trend. Long-term leasing of production equipment by industry has established itself as a major new form of business financing among industrial distributors.

The trend to *specialization* will most likely continue. The reason this branch of distribution should see sustained growth is that it is easier for new firms to start as specialists rather than as general line firms. Investment capital needed is considerably lower. A former mill supplies salesman may have specialized knowledge about one field which is in much demand in his territory and he can often enlist manufacturer support in setting up a specialized distributorship.

POTENTIAL

Industrial distributors who are members of the National and Southern Industrial Distributors Associations (NIDA/SIDA) reported approximately $2.5 billion in total sales during 1976. Most industrial distributors are small, independent businesses, although some are large-scale public corporations with many branches. The sales of an "average" industrial distributor will total about $2.5 million annually, according to NIDA/SIDA. Typical industrial distributors handling general lines will average from 20,000 to 30,000 different items in their inventory. This figure may range from 5,000 items for a distributor specializing in certain product lines to as many as 50,000 different items for the larger firms. NIDA/SIDA indicate that the gross margin has traditionally averaged between 22% and 24% of sales, and net profit as a percentage of net worth (return on investment, or ROI) averaged 15.24% for NIDA members during 1975.

The market for sales through industrial distributors is not static, but only limited by the economic forces in the country. Industrial distributors are taking advantage of new markets. For instance, the interest in environmental quality control and energy conservation has opened a whole new market for industrial distributors. Enterprising distributors have set up divisions to handle pollution control equipment.

Industrial distributors have, like others, been subject to mergers and acquisitions. Many have merged to form large corporations. Others have been absorbed by venture-seeking conglomerates. The industrial distributor of the immediate future will be beset with higher operating costs, inflation and a dwindling profit margin. His survival will depend on his ability to grow with the times.

Appendix
Case Example

THE TRANSPORTATION PROBLEM (USING THE "DISTRIBUTION SOLUTION")

The so-called "Transportation Problem" refers to a specific dilemma which requires the allocation of effort to various segments of an operation. As such, it has much broader application than to the problems discussed here. Its early usage in connection with the optimization of transportation costs earned it its name, and it has continued to enjoy its greatest amount of practical use in connection with problems involving transportation and logistics in the allocation of effort. A solution of allocation problems by "linear programming" techniques may require a knowledge of elementary or advanced mathematics, depending on the technique employed. The "distribution solution" to the problem, discussed here, assumes the former (as opposed to the "simplex solution" to an allocation problem, an example of which is covered in the companion volume of this VNR Series, "Management Decision-Making").

The linear programming approach to problems assumes that the most important relationships are exactly or approximately linear in nature. For example, the most common assumption in a shipping point allocation problem is that the transportation costs are linear in relation to volume. That is, costs are twice as much to transport two items as to transport one. It is important to keep this assumption in mind because it offers opportunities for scientific solution at the same time that it imposes important limitations on the ultimate solution it provides.

ORGANIZATION OF INFORMATION

The best way of setting forth the information needed for the distribution approach to the transportation problem is in matrix form. Information for an example situation involving Store Display Equipment, Inc., is shown in Exhibit I.

124 VNR CONCISE GUIDE TO BUSINESS LOGISTICS

Store Display operates four plants producing the same item, store display units, for shipment to four distribution warehouses.

Information necessary for the solution is the prospective cost of production at each plant, plant capacities, demands at each warehouse for a given period of time, and the cost to transport a unit from each plant to each distribution warehouse. The latter, when added to production costs, provides the total cost to land a unit at each warehouse from each plant. An analysis of every origin-destination pair is necessary because no constraints are typically placed on origin-destination pairs at the outset of the solution.

The goal of solutions to the transportation problem is either to maximize or minimize some element of the problem, in this case costs. Whichever is the case, it will determine the way in which information is presented and manipulated in the matrix. The goal in the example discussed here is to minimize total landed costs at the sum of the locations in the distribution system.

In Exhibit I, cost to produce a unit of product at each of the four plants is shown below the plant location. Transportation costs per unit and the total

EXHIBIT I
DEMAND AND SUPPLY PATTERN, LANDED COST PER UNIT, JANUARY, 19——,
STORE DISPLAY EQUIPMENT, INC.

Row	Warehouse	C_1 Jersey City (21)	C_2 Hershey (26)	C_3 Richmond (24)	C_4 Cleveland (24)	Warehouse (Market) Demand (In Units)
R_1	Philadelphia	23 / 2 / M_{11}	27 / 1 / M_{12}	29 / 5 / M_{13}	29 / 5 / M_{14}	30
R_2	Richmond	26 / 5 / M_{21}	31 / 5 / M_{22}	24 / 0 / M_{23}	31 / 7 / M_{24}	20
R_3	Cincinnati	27 / 6 / M_{31}	32 / 6 / M_{32}	30 / 6 / M_{33}	27 / 3 / M_{34}	20
R_4	New York	22 / 1 / M_{41}	27 / 1 / M_{42}	30 / 6 / M_{43}	30 / 6 / M_{44}	90
R_5	Dummy	40 / M_{51}	40 / M_{52}	40 / M_{53}	40 / M_{54}	50
Plant Capacity (In Units):		40	90	30	50	Total 210

KEY: Number in circle = Production cost at each location (dollars).
Number underlined = Transportation cost from each plant to each warehouse (dollars).
Number in box = Total landed cost from each plant to each warehouse (dollars).

landed costs from each plant to each warehouse are indicated in the approximate matrix squares.

The amounts of capacity and demand in the matrix must balance if a solution is to be achieved. Because capacity and demand rarely balance in real situations, it is often necessary to force a balance by adding a "dummy warehouse" (when capacity exceeds expected demand) or a "dummy plant" (when demand exceeds capacity). The former has been done in Exhibit I.

The amount of product assigned to a dummy will never be produced or shipped. Products demanded by a dummy warehouse, for example, will reduce the actual production level of the plant designated to ship to it. The assignment of production to a dummy plant will determine customers who will or will not be served.

When the goal is to maximize something, usually profits, the values for shipments should be set unrealistically low. When the goal of the solution is to minimize costs, as in this case, the cost of shipping dummy warehouses, or from dummy plants, should be set at an arbitrarily-chosen, unrealistically high level. Since actual dummy costs are unknown, they are usually set equal to one another.

THE INITIAL ALLOCATION

To establish a starting point, it is necessary to match up origins and destinations in some manner. This can be done haphazardly. Or one can assign as much product as possible to the matrix square with the lowest cost, the next lowest cost, on until all product has been assigned. Another method is to begin at the "northwest" (upper left hand) corner, assigning as much as possible to matrix square M_{11} and the succeeding squares in the first row, then dropping down to the first available square in the second row to continue assignments.

Any system of initially matching origins and destinations should be designed to shorten subsequent work in effecting the distribution solution to the transportation problem. The best short cut to solving the problem is provided by the "least cost differential" method of assignment. The steps to be carried out are as follows (they are illustrated in Exhibits II and III):

(1) Compute the difference between the least cost and the second to least cost square in each row and column, placing it in the least cost differential column outside each row and column. (See Exhibit II.)

(2) Assign as much product as possible to the least cost square in the row or column with the greatest least cost differential. Enter the amount in the matrix square.

Where there are two differentials with the same value (as in R_4 and C_3 in the first step of the example, shown in Exhibit II), "secondary differentials" must be computed. They consist of a consideration of the amount of extra cost incurred by accepting the second least cost in a row or column if the least cost alternative is made unavailable. Thus, the least-cost market supplied from the Jersey City

Exhibit II
First Step in the Allocation of Demand and Supply, January, 19——, Store Display Equipment, Inc., by the Least Cost Differential Method of Assignment

			C_1	C_2	C_3	C_4	
		Least Cost Differential, First Step	$23 - 22 = 1$	$27 - 27 = 0$	$29 - 24 = 5$	$29 - 27 = 2$	Unallocated Warehouse (Market) Demand (In Units)
	Least Cost Differential, First Step	Warehouse	\multicolumn{4}{c	}{Plant}	
			Jersey City	Hershey	Richmond	Cleveland	
R_1	$27 - 23 = 4$	Philadelphia	23 M_{11}	27 M_{12}	29 M_{13}	29 M_{14}	Before and after assignment = 30
R_2	$26 - 24 = 2$	Richmond	26 M_{21}	31 M_{22}	24 ← 20 M_{23}	31 M_{24}	Before assignment = 20 After assignment = 0
R_3	$27 - 27 = 0$	Cincinnati	27 M_{31}	32 M_{32}	30 M_{33}	27 M_{34}	Before and after assignment = 20
R_4	$27 - 22 = 5$	New York	22 M_{41}	27 M_{42}	30 M_{43}	30 M_{44}	Before and after assignment = 90
R_5	$40 - 40 = 0$	Dummy	40 M_{51}	40 M_{52}	40 M_{53}	40 M_{54}	Before and after assignment = 50
		Unallocated Plant Capacity (In Units):	Before and after assignment = 40	Before and after assignment = 90	Before assignment = 30 After assignment = 10	Before and after assignment = 50	

KEY: Number in box = Cost of shipping one unit between a pair of points indicated by column and row headings (dollars).
M_{11} = Matrix square with coordinates of R_1 (Row No. 1) and C_1 (Column No. 1).
← = Matrix square to which first allocation is made.

plant is New York at $22 per unit. But if it is decided that it is more economical to supply New York from some other plant, the second alternative is to send Jersey City production to Philadelphia at $23 per unit. The secondary differential of R_4 is said to be 1. By the same process, the secondary differential of C_3 is 2, the difference between M_{23} and M_{21}. In those cases where there are "ties" in least cost differentials, allocation should be made to the matrix square with the greatest secondary differential, in this case M_{23}. The amount allocated is 20 units, total demand at Richmond.

APPENDIX 127

(3) Deduct the amount supplied and demanded from plant capacity and warehouse demand, respectively. The amount remaining will be unallocated supply or demand. If a plant's capacity is totally exhausted and/or a warehouse's demand is totally filled by the action, cross out the appropriate row or column to

Exhibit III
Completed Initial Allocation of Demand and Supply, 19——, Store Equipment, Inc., by the Least Cost Differential Method of Assignment

Least Cost Differential (See Key a)			C_1	C_2	C_3	C_4	Unallocated Warehouse (Market) Demand (In Units) (See Key a)
			1-1 5-x 2-1 6-x 3-x 7-x 4-x	1-0 5-13 2-0 6-x 3-0 7-x 4-0	1-5 5-11 2-1 6-x 3-1 7-x 4-1	1-2 5-11 2-2 6-x 3-2 7-x 4-1	
Least Cost Differential (See Key a)		Warehouse	Plant				
			Jersey City	Hershey	Richmond	Cleveland	
R_1	1-4 5-2 2-4 6-x 3-2 7-x 4-2	Philadelphia	23 M_{11}	27 ⑤ 30 M_{12}	29 M_{13}	29 M_{14}	1-30 5-30 2-30 6-x 3-30 7-x 4-30
R_2	1-2 5-x 2-x 6-x 3-x 7-x 4-x	Richmond	26 M_{21}	31 M_{22}	24 ① 20 M_{23}	31 M_{24}	1-20 5-x 2-x 6-x 3-x 7-x 4-x
R_3	1-0 5-x 2-0 6-x 3-3 7-x 4-x	Cincinnati	27 M_{31}	32 M_{32}	30 M_{33}	27 ③ 20 M_{34}	1-20 5-x 2-20 6-x 3-20 7-x 4-x
R_4	1-5 5-x 2-5 6-x 3-3 7-x 4-3	New York	22 ② 40 M_{41}	27 ④ 50 M_{42}	30 M_{43}	30 M_{44}	1-90 5-x 2-90 6-x 3-50 7-x 4-50
R_5	1-0 5-0 2-0 6-0 3-0 7-x 4-0	Dummy	40 M_{51}	40 ⑥ 10 M_{52}	40 ⑥ 10 M_{53}	40 ⑥ 30 M_{54}	1-50 5-50 2-50 6-x 3-50 7-x 4-50
		Unallocated Plant Capacity (In Units)	1-40 2-40 3-x 4-x 5-x 6-x 7-x	1-90 2-90 3-90 4-90 5-40 6-10 7-x	1-30 2-10 3-10 4-10 5-10 6-10 7-x	1-50 2-50 3-50 4-30 5-30 6-30 7-x	Total 210

KEY a: 1-2, 2-x, etc. = Results of successive calculations of least cost differentials, unallocated plant capacity, and unsatisfied warehouse demand for each row and column (number before dash indicates step; number after dash indicates results of calculation).

x = Capacity totally accounted for or demand fully satisfied, thereby eliminating the need to compute a least cost differential for the respective row or column.

Number in box = Cost of shipping one unit between a pair of points indicated by column and row headings (dollars).

M_{11} = Matrix square with coordinates of R_1 (Row No. 1) and C_1 (Column No. 1).

Number in circle = The order of the initial allocation of supply to demand. Underlined quantities indicate the amounts so allocated.

eliminate it from further consideration. In Exhibit III, for example, this has been accomplished by placing an "x" in the least cost differential notation for R_2 opposite step number two.

(4) Recompute least cost differentials and make the second assignment of product to an origin-destination pair.

(5) When all plant capacities and warehouse demands have been exhausted except those in the dummy row (or column), allocate the remaining capacity and demand in the final step (step number seven in the example).

The completed initial allocation of demand and supply by the least cost differential method of assignment is shown in Exhibit III. The total cost of the first allocation is computed in the table, Exhibit IV. It is $4,060. To determine whether or not it is the lowest that can be found, it is necessary to check the matrix.

MATRIX CHECK

We must create an artificial set of values for the purpose of checking the matrix. To do this, we can set any row or column matrix check value equal to any amount we wish. Generally, to simplify matters, R_1 is set equal to zero. The remaining matrix check values are set relative to it by equating each matrix square value (cost) to which items have been allocated to the sum of matrix check values for its row and column. In Exhibit V, this is achieved by the following process:

EXHIBIT IV
TOTAL COST OF FIRST ALLOCATION,
JANUARY, 19——, STORE DISPLAY EQUIPMENT, INC.

Origin-Destination	Landed Cost Per Unit	Units	Total Landed Cost
Richmond-Richmond	$24	20	$480
Jersey City-New York	22	40	880
Cleveland-Cincinnati	27	20	540
Hershey-New York	27	50	1,350
Hershey-Philadelphia	27	30	810
Hershey-Dummy	40	10	Not Shipped
Richmond-Dummy	40	10	Not Shipped
Cleveland-Dummy	40	30	Not Shipped
		210	$4,060

Exhibit V
Matrix Check of Alternative Initial Allocation, January, 19——, Store Display Equipment, Inc.

Matrix Check Values	Warehouse	$C_1 = 22$ Jersey City	$C_2 = 27$ Hershey	$C_3 = 27$ Richmond	$C_4 = 27$ Cleveland	Warehouse Demand
$R_1 = 0$	Philadelphia	23 | +1[a] M_{11}	27 | 0 30[b] M_{12}	29 | +2 M_{13}	29 | +2 M_{14}	30
$R_2 = 4$	Richmond	26 | 0 M_{21}	31 | 0 M_{22}	24 | −7 M_{23}	31 | 0 M_{24} 20	20
$R_3 = 3$	Cincinnati	27 | +2 M_{31}	32 | +2 M_{32}	30 | 0 20 M_{33}	27 | −3 M_{34}	20
$R_4 = 0$	New York	22 | 0 40 M_{41}	27 | 0 50 M_{42}	30 | +3 M_{43}	30 | +3 M_{44}	90
$R_5 = 13$	Dummy	40 | +5 M_{51}	40 | 0 M_{52} 10	40 | 0 M_{53} 10	40 | 0 M_{54} 30	50
	Plant Capacities	40	90	30	50	210

[a] Number in the upper right-hand corner of each matrix square denotes the relationship of the square's value to the sum of matrix check values for its row and column coordinates.

[b] Underlined quantities indicate the amounts (in units) allocated to each destination from each origin.

$$R_1 = 0$$
$$R_1\,(0) + C_2\,(?) = 27;\ C_2 = 27$$
$$C_2\,(27) + R_4\,(?) = 27;\ R_4 = 0$$
$$R_4\,(0) + C_1\,(?) = 22;\ C_1 = 22$$
$$\text{etc.}$$

Matrix check values were obtained by using the "stepping stones" (squares to which items were allocated in the theoretical body of water represented by the remaining unoccupied squares in the matrix.) The values are next checked against "water" squares to determine if the first allocation is optimum (least cost). In each case, the sum of R and C matrix check values should not exceed the value of the matrix water square defined by each row and column. Saying it another way, we must ask ourselves:

$$\text{Is } R_1 + C_1 > M_{11}?$$
$$0 + 22 > 23?\quad \text{No.}$$

If not, as in this case, we proceed to the next set of R and C values, and their matrix square. The matrix square (M_{11}) in question indicates no reallocation is necessary to optimize the solution.

Whenever a matrix square is encountered that has a cost value less than the sum of its R and C matrix check values, a lower cost solution could be obtained by allocating some product to it. Even after encountering such a situation, it is best to check all of the "water" squares in the matrix first; for the one whose cost value is the greatest amount less than the sum of its R and C matrix check values will offer the greatest cost reduction through the reallocation of freight to it. It thus provides us with a starting point in optimizing the final allocation.

REALLOCATION

There are no set rules in making an initial allocation of supply to demand; one need only adhere to restrictions imposed by facility capacities and demand quantities. The modified distribution method outlined above is only an approach which helps eliminate further reallocation and adjustments to produce an optimum solution. We could have just as well employed a technique which produced an allocation such as that shown in Exhibit V. How do we go about making necessary adjustments to optimize it, assuming we have no previous knowledge of information in Exhibit III?

First it is necessary to perform the same check on "stone" and "water" squares as described above. Our check reveals negative water values for matrix squares M_{23} and M_{34}. One need not check all matrix squares; instead, the first negative square encountered can provide the focal point for the first reallocation effort. However, the square with the most negative difference between matrix check value sums and total cost will produce the greatest savings and progress if reallocation is based upon it. In Exhibit V, square M_{23} yields the highest negative value of − 7.

From the most negative water square, trace a path on the matrix using only stone squares as points at which to make 90-degree angles. The path will resemble a series of moves that might be made by a chess rook with the provision that the rook must come to rest only on stone squares and proceed at a 90-degree angle on its next move. The object is to trace a path back to the starting water square. Stone squares can be passed over by a given move. There is no specified number of moves necessary to return the pathmaker to his "home" water square. Because of its resemblance to the technique employed by a person crossing a bridgeless creek, this method of reallocation is referred to as the "stepping stone" method. The path resulting from the application of this technique to the above problem is shown also in Exhibit V.

Because of the requirement that the path include only 90-degree turns, there will always be an even number of moves in any path. In the example, there are four. Each of these moves should next be assigned alternate plus and minus signs beginning from the first. Next, subtract the smallest quantity allocated to a stone square in which a positive move is terminated from all other stone squares at which positive moves are terminated. Likewise, add this same quantity to each square, be it stone or water, at which a negative move is terminated. In Exhibit V, this results in a reallocation of ten units from squares M_{53} and M_{24} to squares M_{54} ans M_{23}. In terms of dollar savings, this can be translated to $70. (Ten units supplied at a cost of $24 per unit rather than $31.) A second matrix check would tell us that this is not yet an optimum solution to the problem.

Two more iterations of the reallocation procedure would be required to produce the same result shown in Exhibit III. The first of these would result in the deduction of ten units each from squares M_{24} and M_{33} and the addition of the same amounts to squares M_{23} and M_{34}. The second iteration would reallocate ten units from squares M_{54} and M_{33} to squares M_{34} and M_{53}. (The reader may wish to carry out these subsequent reallocations in order to check his understanding of the procedure.) Based on this example, the importance of initial care in allocating supply to demand should be clear.

INTRODUCTION OF CONSTRAINTS

Constraints such as, "Always work the Hershey plant to capacity, regardless of cost," "Never ship to Cincinnati from Cleveland," or "Always meet the demands of the New York warehouse" (or more typically a given customer), are sometimes introduced into allocation problems. They require only minor alterations in the initial formulation of data to solve a problem. Consider the second of the constraints imposed above on the Store Display Equipment, Inc., example.

In order to discourage the allocation of goods to Cincinnati from Cleveland, we need only to set the cost value of square M_{34} in Exhibit III arbitrarily and artificially high and proceed to solve the matrix once again. Any high number might be chosen, although theoretically there is no absolute minimum quantity that will quarantee compliance with the constraint. Therefore, the safest recommendation would be to assign the largest possible value, designated by any symbol (Z will do), to M_{34} and solve as if it were a number, albeit a very large one. Other adjustments of a similar type can be made to meet any of the above limitations which might be imposed for either rational or irrational reasons.

ALTERNATE SOLUTIONS

A given optimum solution may be undesirable for a number of reasons. But most allocation problems have several optimum (basic) or near-optimum solutions offering an alternate operating plan at little or no cost over minimum. Whether or not a problem has more than one basic solution can be determined by a check of the water squares similar to that performed to determine optimality. For every water square with a cost value equivalent to the sum of its R and C matrix check values (i.e., a water square value = 0), there will be an alternate optimum or basic solution. (If there are two or more of these, it can be demonstrated that there are an infinite number of quantities in which goods can be allocated to the several routes, all of which yield an optimum total result.)

Degeneracy. For any given matrix there is an exact number of stone squares which will allow a solution. It is one less than the sum of the number of rows and columns in the matrix, or $R + C - 1$. There is no guarantee that an initial allocation, even by a formal method, will produce the desired number of stone squares. There may be either too many or too few. They should be counted after the initial allocation and before solution. If not discovered, however, an incorrect number will soon halt the solution procedure after some wasted effort on the part of the analyst.

When an initial allocation produced too many stone squares, alternatives will be introduced in the assignment of matrix check values to rows and columns, obscuring the one best method. When this is the case, stone square allocations should be combined to produce the desired number before any attempt is made to check the solution for optimality.

Degeneracy results from the presence of too few stone squares in a matrix, either after an initial allocation or as the result of allocation procedures. In either case, a degenerate situation will not allow matrix check values to be assigned to all rows and columns. It can be corrected by arbitrarily allocating 0 units to any matrix square, thus creating the necessary stone or stones to facilitate the establishment of matrix check values. The actual square to be selected will have to fall in one row or one column of the matrix. The best of the possible squares to convert from water to a stone is that which best accomplishes the objective of the solution. In the Store Display Equipment, Inc., example it would be the one with the lowest cost value. Once a new stone square has been created, the problem should be solved in the normal manner, regarding the matrix square with 0 units assigned to it as one would any other stone square.

Occasionally, a deficiency of stone squares is created during solution. This will occur when reallocation converts one more stone square to water than vice-versa. It requires the allocation of 0 units, as above, to one of the stone squares eliminated by the allocation. The one to select for conversion from water back to a stone is once again the one which best accomplishes the desired goal. Once this has been achieved, the solution can proceed as before.

Solution by Computer. Rarely does a problem lend itself to a manual linear programming analysis. Because the complexity of the calculations required to solve larger matrices grows geometrically in relation to the increase in size of the matrix, computers invariably are employed to carry out such calculations. Nevertheless, it is useful to understand the logic underlying such calculations, and to be aware of the assumptions implicit in the use of linear programming by the transportation method.

Index

Index

"ABC" analysis in inventory
    management, 69

Bonded warehousing, 114
Business logistics, approaches and
    techniques, 1-6
    definition, xi
    and mathematical programming, 4

Containerization, 91, 104
Conveyors, 55

Economic order quantities, 62-67, 72
    chart for, 66, 75
Entrepreneurial districts, 23

Freight forwarders, 92, 94
Forklift trucks, 56

General Electric Company, re value
    engineering, 36
    re vendor rating, 44

Industrial distributors, 116-121
    definition, 116
    trends in, 119
Industrial districts, 22-29
    community-sponsored, 23
    industry-sponsored, 23
    office districts, 28
    railroad-sponsored, 23
    for research and development, 26
Inventory management, 60-76
    "ABC" analysis in, 69
    cushions for, 61

economic order quantities in, 62-67, 72
and purchasing, 33
reorder points in, 70
    chart for, 75
    and Poisson distribution, 70, 72
stockout policy for, 71, 72
(*See also* Material management)

Labor costs, and plant location, 13-16

Material management, 49-59
    equipment for, 52-58
    organization for, 51
    planning for, 58
    and "processing on the move," 54
    trade-offs in, 50
    and unit load concept, 57
    (*See also* Inventory management)
Mathematical programming, 4
Monorail systems, 55

National Association of Purchasing
    Agents, 31, 32

Office districts, 28

Packaging, 97-106
    color standards for, 102
    for containerized shipping, 104
    development and engineering, 100
    organization for, 97
    for protection, 103
    quality control in, 102
    research for, 99
    scope of, 98-103

INDEX

Packaging (*Cont.*)
  specifications for, 101
  testing of, 101
  and "unitization," 105
  value analysis for, 103
Physical distribution management, 77–96
  (*See also* Traffic Management, Transportation)
Plant location, 7–21
  checklist for, 19
  and labor costs, 13–16
  and pollution, 16
  and transportation costs, 10
  and warehouse location, 13
Poisson distribution in inventory management, 70, 72
Pollution, and plant location, 16
Pre-production purchase analysis, 32
Public warehousing, 110–114
Purchasing, 29–35
  administrative costs of, 35
  and inventory control, 33
  reorder points in, 70, 72, 75
  vendor evaluation in, 33
  (*See also* Value engineering, Value analysis)

Quality control in packaging, 102

Railroad districts, 23
Research and development districts, 28

Shippers' associations, 94–96
Stockouts, in inventory management, 71, 73

Traffic management, 79–96
  and common carriers, 86
  and contract carriers, 86
  for freight transportation, 80
  organization for, 82
  and regulation of carriers, 86
  services for, 92–96
  for smaller companies, 85
  (*See also* Transportation)
Transportation, containerization for, 91
  modes of, 88–91
    costs of, 90
  and plant location, 13
  regulation of, 86–88
  structure of the transportation industry, 86–92
  (*See also* Traffic management)
The Transportation Problem, case example, 123–133

Unit-load concept, in material management, 57

Value engineering (Value analysis), 32, 36–43
  definition, 37
  methodology, 38
  and Navy Bureau of Ships, 37
  organization for, 42
  proposal development for, 40
  recent developments in, 41
  and the value engineer, 43
  (*See also* Purchasing)
Vendor rating, 33, 44–48

Warehousing, 107–115
  bonded, 114
  location, 13
  public, 110–114
  trade-offs in, 108